Career Discovery Encyclopedia

Sixth Edition

Career Discovery Encyclopedia

Sixth Edition

VOLUME 3

Costume Designers
Food Production Workers

Ferguson
An imprint of Infobase Publishing

Career Discovery Encyclopedia, Sixth Edition

Ferguson
An imprint of Infobase Publishing
132 West 31st Street
New York NY 10001

Library of Congress Cataloging-in-Publication Data

Career discovery encyclopedia.—6th ed.
    p. cm.
  Includes Bibliographical references and indexes.
  Summary: In 8 volumes presents articles describing over 650 jobs or career fields, discussing personal, educational, and professional requirements; ways of exploring the career; salary statistics; job outlook; and how to obtain more information about the career.
  ISBN 0-8160-6696-5 (hc : alk. paper)
  1. Vocational guidance—Dictionaries, Juvenile. I. J.G. Ferguson Publishing Company.
  HF5381.2.C37 2006
  331.70203—dc22   2006005575

Text design by Erika K. Arroyo
Cover design by Salvatore Luongo

Printed in the United States of America

EB EJB 10 9 8 7 6 5 4 3 2 1

This book is printed on acid-free paper.

Contents

0580 7591

Career Cluster Icons

Agriculture, Food, and Natural Resources

Hospitality and Tourism

Architecture and Construction

Human Services

Arts, Audio-Video Technology, and Communication

Information Technology

Business, Management, and Administration

Law, Public Safety, and Security

Education and Training

Manufacturing

Finance

Marketing, Sales, and Service

Government and Public Administration

Science, Technology, Engineering, and Mathematics

Health Science

Transportation, Distribution, and Logistics

CAREER ARTICLES

Costume Designers

What Costume Designers Do

Costume designers create the costumes seen in the theater, on television, and in the movies. They also design costumes for figure skaters, ballroom dancers, and other performers. During the planning of a show, costume designers read the script. They meet with directors to decide what types of costumes each character should wear for each scene.

Stories that take place in the past are called period pieces. For these shows, costume designers must have a great deal of knowledge about what people wore during different historical time periods in different parts of the world. Designers do research at libraries, museums, and universities. They study the garments, shoes, hats, belts, bags, and jewelry worn by men, women, and children. They look at the colors and types of fabric and study how garments were made. Costume designers might use ideas that come from looking at the fashion details of the specific historical, modern, or future era in which the show is set. Once

the research is finished, designers begin to make sketches of their costume ideas. They try to design each outfit so that it looks authentic, or similar to something that would have actually been worn in the time period when the story occurs.

Costume designers meet with directors to get their designs approved. They also meet with stage designers and art directors to make sure that the furniture and backdrops do not clash with the costumes. They meet with lighting designers to make sure that the lighting will not change the appearance of costume colors.

Costume designers decide whether to rent, purchase, or sew the costumes. They shop for clothing and accessories, fabrics, and sewing supplies. They also supervise assistants who do the sewing.

Education and Training

To become a costume designer, you will need at least a high school diploma. To prepare for a career in this field, begin

SCHOOL SUBJECTS
Family and consumer science,
   Theater/dance

MINIMUM EDUCATION LEVEL
High school diploma

SALARY RANGE
$15,000 to $22,000 to $37,000

OUTLOOK
Decline

OTHER ARTICLES TO READ
Artists
Fashion Coordinators
Fashion Designers
Fashion Illustrators and Photographers
Stage Production Workers
Tailors and Dressmakers

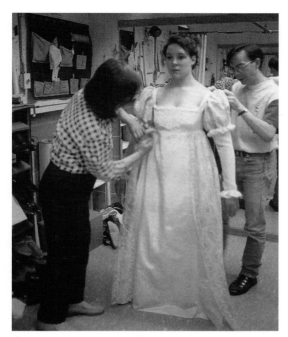

A costume designer works on an elaborate costume that will reflect the personality of the character wearing it.

entertainment business is dependent on the health of the overall economy. Many theaters, especially small and nonprofit theaters, are cutting their budgets or doing smaller shows that require fewer costumes.

Nevertheless, opportunities for costume designers exist. Costume designers are able to work in an increasing number of locations as new regional theaters and cable and production television companies operate throughout the United States and Canada.

For More Information

To prepare for a career as a costume designer, join a school drama club, a dance troupe, or a community theater and volunteer to work on costumes or props. Learn to sew using commercial patterns, or try making some of your original designs.

The Costumer's Handbook and *The Costume Designer's Handbook,* both by Rosemary Ingham and Elizabeth Covey, are good resources for beginning or experienced costume designers.

Costume Designers Guild
4730 Woodman Avenue, Suite 430
Sherman Oaks, CA 91423
818-905-1557
cdgia@earthlink.net
http://www.costumedesignersguild.com

Costume Society of America
55 Edgewater Drive
PO Box 73
Earleville, MD 21919
800-272-9447
http://www.costumesocietyamerica.com

National Costumers Association
6914 Upper Trail Circle
Mesa, AZ 85207-0943
800-622-1321
http://www.costumers.org

by taking a wide range of classes in high school. English and literature courses will help you read and understand scripts. History classes are helpful for researching historical costumes and time periods. Courses in sewing, art, designing, and draping are also necessary. Mathematics classes will help you master sewing patterns, and family and consumer science classes will also be helpful. Earning a college degree in costume design, fashion design, or fiber art and obtaining experience working in theater or film are also helpful.

Outlook

It is predicted that employment for tailors, dressmakers, and skilled sewers will decline through 2012, and costume designers may not do much better. The health of the

Counter and Retail Clerks

What Counter and Retail Clerks Do

Counter and retail clerks take orders and collect payments for a wide variety of businesses. They are the public representatives of businesses that provide goods and services. Counter and retail clerks work in supermarkets, drugstores, convenience stores, cleaners, computer shops, athletic and footwear boutiques, photo-finishing stores, and many other types of businesses. Many counter and retail clerks work in the rental industry. They may work as clerks at a car rental agency at an airport, in video stores, or at other establishments that rent goods or services to the consumer.

Counter and retail clerks take orders and collect payments from the public. They keep records of receipts using a cash register or computer terminal. They are responsible for keeping track of the money in their register throughout the day and making sure that the amount is correct when the shift is over. Clerks also bag or wrap the customers' purchases and sometimes arrange for their delivery. Counter and retail clerks are sometimes responsible for the display and presentation of products in their store. They may clean shelves or sweep floors, if necessary. In supermarkets and grocery stores, clerks stock shelves and bag food purchases for customers.

In smaller shops with no sales staff, or in a situation when a salesperson is unavailable, counter and retail clerks assist customers with purchases or rentals. They may locate and demonstrate the merchandise as well as answer the customers' questions.

There are many examples of the wide variety of counter and retail clerks. *Video and DVD rental clerks* greet customers, check out tapes, and accept payment. When the customers return their rentals, the clerks check the condition of the tapes and put them back onto the shelves. *Equipment-rental clerks* prepare rental forms and quote rates to customers. They answer customer questions about the operation of the equipment. They often take a deposit to cover any accidents or possible damage.

SCHOOL SUBJECTS
Business, Mathematics, Speech

MINIMUM EDUCATION LEVEL
High school diploma

SALARY RANGE
$13,000 to $18,000 to $34,000

OUTLOOK
Faster than the average

OTHER ARTICLES TO READ
Bank Services Workers
Cashiers
Clerks
Retail Sales Workers
Sales Representatives
Supermarket Managers and Workers

When the customers return the equipment, clerks check it to make certain it is in good working order. *Shoe repair shop clerks* receive shoes that need to be cleaned or repaired. They examine the shoes, quote a price, and give the customer a receipt.

Education and Training

There are no formal educational requirements necessary for becoming a counter and retail clerk. In high school, take classes in business, mathematics, English, and speech. Knowledge of a foreign language may allow you to have more job options. Most employers like to hire high school graduates, but there are many jobs available for those who are still in school.

This retail clerk is assisting a customer with a jewelry purchase.

Outlook

It is predicted that employment for counter and retail clerks will grow faster than the average through 2012. Businesses that focus on customer service will always want to hire friendly and responsible clerks. Major employers should be those that provide rental products and services, such as car rental firms, video and DVD rental stores, and other equipment rental businesses. Many job openings will come from the need to replace workers. Opportunities for temporary or part-time work should be good, especially during busy business periods. There are many employment opportunities for clerks in large metropolitan areas.

For More Information

To prepare for a career as a counter and retail clerk, get a part-time job in the industry. Visit the National Retail Federation's Web site (listed following this paragraph) for a list of colleges and universities offering degrees in retail merchandising, retail sales, and other related subjects. Visit http://www.retailworker.com for news on the retail industry and a free newsletter.

International Mass Retail Association
1700 North Moore Street, Suite 2250
Arlington, VA 22209
703-841-2300
http://www.imra.org

National Retail Federation
325 7th Street, NW, Suite 1100
Washington, DC 20004
800-673-4692
http://www.nrf.com

United Food & Commercial Workers International Union
AFL-CIO/CLC
1775 K Street, NW
Washington, DC 20006
202-223-3111
http://www.ufcw.org

Court Reporters

SKILLS SPOTLIGHT

◆

What they do
Evaluate and manage information
Communicate ideas
Select and apply tools/technology

Skills they need
Reading/writing
Responsibility
Speaking/listening

What Court Reporters Do

Court reporters keep track of everything that is said at hearings and trials. This information is called testimony. Court reporters use symbols to rapidly record this testimony. The collection of these symbols is called shorthand.

In a courtroom, people may speak between 250 and 300 words per minute. Court reporters must record each word that is spoken. A stenotype machine is used to do this. A stenotype machine has a keyboard with 24 keys. There is a symbol on each key. Each symbol or combination of symbols stands for a sound, word, or a phrase. As testimony is given, the court reporter records it by striking the proper keys. The symbols are printed on a strip of paper and recorded on a computer disk.

Because court reporters make the official record of trials, they cannot miss a word or phrase. If this happens, the court reporter must interrupt the trial and ask to have the words repeated. The judge sometimes asks the court reporter to read aloud testimony that has already been recorded.

Court reporters use computers to help them in their work. Computer programs (called computer-aided transcription programs) are used to change the symbols and words of a stenotype machine into standard English. The computer can then print out a record of the trial. That way, the reporter does not have to retype it or read it into a tape recorder.

The court reporter's job does not stop in the courtroom. The court reporter must edit and proofread the transcript (the printed version of the testimony) because the computer program produces only a rough draft of the text. After the court reporter edits the text, the transcript is copied, bound in a durable binder, and sent on to the lawyers and the judge.

Most court reporters work in city, county, state, or federal courts. Some work for private companies, where they record business meetings and conventions. Others work for freelance reporting companies

SCHOOL SUBJECTS
English, Government

MINIMUM EDUCATION LEVEL
Some postsecondary training

SALARY RANGE
$23,000 to $42,000 to $81,000

OUTLOOK
About as fast as the average

OTHER ARTICLES TO READ
Interpreters and Translators
Legal Secretaries
Paralegals
Real-Time Captioners
Secretaries
Stenographers

that provide reporters for trials and business meetings.

Education and Training

Court reporters are required to obtain a high school diploma and complete a two- to four-year training program in shorthand reporting. At this program, you will learn how to type at least 225 words a minute on a stenotype machine. You will also study typing, English, law, and medical and legal terms. Programs in shorthand reporting are offered at community colleges, at business and vocational schools, and at some universities.

Outlook

Employment of court reporters will grow about as fast as the average for all occupations through 2012. The rising number of criminal court cases and civil lawsuits will cause both state and federal court systems to expand. Court reporters can also find work using their skills to produce captioning for television programs, which is a federal requirement for all new television programming by 2006.

For More Information

To get an idea of what a court reporter does, attend trials at your local courts and keep an eye on the court reporter. If you can, watch several reporters in different courtrooms. Observing the reporters under different judges will help you get a perspective on what the average court reporter does. Try to arrange a one-on-one meeting with a court reporter so you can ask questions about his job.

A court reporter records testimony during a trial.

National Court Reporters Association
8224 Old Courthouse Road
Vienna, VA 22182-3808
800-272-6272
http://www.verbatimreporters.com

National Verbatim Reporters Association
2729 Drake Street
PMB 130
Fayetteville, AR 72703
479-582-2200
http://www.nvra.org

United States Court Reporters Association
PO Box 465
Chicago, IL 60690-0465
http://www.uscra.org

Creative Arts Therapists

SKILLS SPOTLIGHT

◆

What they do
Evaluate and manage information
Manage people
Work with a team

Skills they need
Creative thinking
Social
Speaking/listening

What Creative Arts Therapists Do

Creative arts therapists, whom are a subset of *recreational therapists,* help rehabilitate people with mental, physical, and emotional disabilities. They usually work as part of a health care team of physicians, nurses, psychiatrists, psychologists, and social workers. Therapists work in hospitals, schools, rehabilitation centers, nursing homes, and shelters for battered women. They also work in substance abuse programs and correctional facilities. Hospices, which are care centers for terminally ill patients, employ creative arts therapists as well. Some therapists have their own private practices.

The goal of creative arts therapists is to improve their patients' physical, mental, and emotional states. Before they begin any treatment, creative arts therapists meet with a team of other health care professionals. Once they determine the strengths, limitations, and interests of a patient, they create a special program for him or her. Creative arts therapists continue to meet with the other health care workers throughout the course of the program. They may change the program according to the patient's progress. How these goals are reached depends on the unique specialty of the therapist.

There are several types of creative arts therapists. *Music therapists* use music lessons and activities to improve a patient's self-confidence. Playing a musical instrument can help a patient's depression and improve physical ability. *Art therapists* teach patients to express their thoughts, feelings, and worries through sketching, drawing, painting, or sculpting. *Dance and movement therapists* teach dance exercises to help improve the physical, mental, and emotional health of patients. *Drama therapists* use role-playing, puppetry, and performance to increase self-confidence. They also use pantomime, which is the telling of a story by the use of expressive body or facial movements. They also use improvisation, which is unplanned speech or movements, to help patients express themselves. *Poetry therapists* and *bibliotherapists* teach patients

SCHOOL SUBJECTS
Art, Music, Theater/dance

MINIMUM EDUCATION LEVEL
Bachelor's degree

SALARY RANGE
$20,000 to $33,000 to $51,000

OUTLOOK
More slowly than the average

OTHER ARTICLES TO READ
Actors
Artists
Child Life Specialists
Horticultural Therapists
Hypnotherapists
Musicians
Recreational Therapists

A creative arts therapist leads a group through a movement exercise.

to write and speak about their experiences and feelings. This is a powerful way to get rid of anxiety, depression, and fear.

Education and Training

If you are interested in becoming a creative arts therapist, you should begin studying the arts as early as possible. Classes in art, art history, drama, music, and writing will give you important background skills for whichever arts field interests you. English, mathematics, science, and speech classes are also important.

A bachelor's degree is the minimum requirement to become a creative arts therapist. Usually a creative arts therapist earns an undergraduate degree in art, music, or drama and then continues in a master's program. Many colleges and universities offer degrees in specific creative arts therapy fields. A master's degree in education, counseling, or a related field is also acceptable.

Outlook

Overall employment for creative arts therapists is expected to grow more slowly than the average through 2012. Employment in hospitals is expected to decline as many therapeutic services shift to outpatient settings to reduce costs. Job openings in facilities such as nursing homes, however, should continue to increase as the elderly population grows over the next few decades.

For More Information

Volunteer at a hospital, clinic, nursing home, or health care facility to learn about what people with disabilities need. You can also get experience by working at a summer camp for children with disabilities. Take music, art, drama, or dance lessons offered in your community.

American Art Therapy Association
1202 Allanson Road
Mundelein, IL 60060-3808
888-290-0878
http://www.arttherapy.org

American Dance Therapy Association
2000 Century Plaza, Suite 108
10632 Little Patuxent Parkway
Columbia, MD 21044
410-997-4040
http://www.adta.org

American Music Therapy Association
8455 Colesville Road, Suite 1000
Silver Spring, MD 20910
301-589-3300
http://www.musictherapy.org

National Association for Drama Therapy
733 15th Street, NW, Suite 330
Washington, DC 20005
202-966-7409
http://www.nadt.org

National Association for Poetry Therapy
733 15th Street, NW, Suite 330
Washington, DC 20005
http://www.poetrytherapy.org

Credit Analysts

What Credit Analysts Do

Credit analysts analyze financial information to evaluate the amount of risk involved in lending money to businesses or individuals. They contact banks, credit associations, and others to obtain credit information and prepare a written report of findings used to recommend credit limits.

Credit analysts usually concentrate on one of two different areas. *Commercial and business analysts* evaluate risks in business loans. *Consumer credit analysts* evaluate personal loan risks. In both cases an analyst studies financial documents, such as statements of assets and liabilities submitted by the person or company seeking the loan. Credit analysts consult with banks and other financial institutions that have had previous financial relationships with the applicant. Credit analysts prepare, analyze, and approve loan requests and help borrowers fill out applications.

The amount of work involved in a credit check depends on the size and type of the loan requested. Credit analysts check financial statements for all sizes and types of loans, but a larger loan requires a much closer look at economic trends to determine if there is a market for the product being produced and the likelihood of the business failing.

Many credit analysts work only with commercial loans. In studying a commercial loan application, a credit analyst needs to find out if the business or corporation is well managed and financially secure and if the existing economic climate is favorable for the operation's success. He or she examines balance sheets and operating statements to determine the assets and liabilities of a company, its net sales, and its profits or losses. A background check of the applicant company's leading officials is also done to determine if they personally have any outstanding loans.

Analyzing economic trends to determine market conditions is another responsibility of credit analysts who compute dozens of ratios to show how successful the

SCHOOL SUBJECTS
Business, Mathematics

MINIMUM EDUCATION LEVEL
Bachelor's degree

SALARY RANGE
$19,000 to $28,000 to $44,000

OUTLOOK
Decline

OTHER ARTICLES TO READ
Accountants
Auditors
Bank Services Workers
Bookkeepers
Economists
Financial Analysts
Insurance Claims Representatives

company is in relation to similar businesses. Profit-and-loss statements, collection procedures, and other factors are analyzed. This ratio analysis can also be used to measure how successful a particular industry is likely to be, given existing market considerations. Computer programs are used to highlight economic trends and interpret other important data.

The credit analyst always provides a findings report to bank executives, including a complete financial history of the applicant and a recommendation on the loan amount that should be advanced.

Two credit analysts analyze financial information.

Education and Training

Take courses in math, economics, business, computers, and accounting in high school.

Credit analysts usually have at least a bachelor's degree in accounting, finance, or business administration. Those who want to move up in the field often go on to obtain master's degrees in one of these subjects. Undergraduate course work should include business management, economics, statistics, and accounting. Some employers provide new hires with on-the-job training involving both classroom work and hands-on experience.

Outlook

Employment in this field is expected to decline through 2012. Despite an anticipated increase in the number of credit applications, technology will allow these applications to be processed, checked, and authorized by fewer workers than in the past.

Job security for credit analysts is also affected by the local economy and business climate. However, loans are a major source of income for banks, and credit officers are less likely to lose their jobs in an economic downturn.

For More Information

The Credit Management Information and Support Web site (http://www.creditworthy.com) offers interviews with people in the field and advice for breaking into the business. This site also has a section that describes educational resources and offers an online course in the basics of business credit.

Bank Administration Institute
One North Franklin, Suite 1000
Chicago, IL 60606-3421
800-224-9889
http://www.bai.org

Credit Research Foundation
8840 Columbia 100 Parkway
Columbia, MD 21045
410-740-5499
http://www.crfonline.org

National Association of Credit Management
8840 Columbia 100 Parkway
Columbia, MD 21045
410-740-5560
http://www.nacm.org

Crime Analysts

What Crime Analysts Do

Crime analysts try to uncover and piece together information about crime patterns, crime trends, and criminal suspects. A crime analyst collects crime data from many sources. Sources include police reports, statewide computer databases, interviews with suspects, and others. Crime analysts also study general factors such as population density, economic conditions (average income and job availability), and crime reporting practices. They then analyze this information. Crime analysts are constantly on the lookout for details that may create patterns. These patterns can help them track and predict criminal activity.

The activities of the crime analyst can change from day to day. One day, for example, an analyst may meet with the police chief to discuss a string of local car thefts. Another day the analyst may work at the computer, gathering statistics. Sometimes the work includes going on "ride-alongs" with street cops or visiting a crime scene. Crime analysts also sometimes meet with analysts from surrounding areas to exchange information. Occasionally, a crime analyst may be pulled off everyday duties to work exclusively on a task force, usually focusing on a cluster of violent crimes. Crime analysts also monitor activities of people who have criminal reputations, or known offenders such as parolees.

There are three types of analysis: tactical, strategic, and administrative. Tactical crime analysis provides police officers and detectives with fast, relevant information. This is the type of "hot" information that allows police to set up stakeouts and may lead to the arrest of a criminal. Tactical analysis is also used to identify suspects for certain crimes based on their criminal records.

Strategic analysis deals with finding solutions to long-range problems. For example, an analyst might perform a study to see if the police department is making the best use of its staff. The analyst would then offer suggestions for improvement.

SCHOOL SUBJECTS
Computer science, Government, Psychology

MINIMUM EDUCATION LEVEL
Bachelor's degree

SALARY RANGE
$30,000 to $59,000 to $92,000

OUTLOOK
About as fast as the average

OTHER ARTICLES TO READ
Deputy U.S. Marshals
Detectives
F.B.I Agents
Fire Inspectors and Investigators
Forensic Experts
Police Officers

Crime analysts rely on computers to sort through thousands of pieces of data to help them solve crimes.

Administrative analysis provides statistical information and policy recommendations to those in charge of a police department. This analysis may include a study on the activity levels and current labor force levels of police officers.

Education and Training

While you are in high school, you can prepare for a career as a crime analyst by taking English and speech classes that will develop your communication as well as research skills. Math classes, such as algebra, will help you in understanding statistics. Basic knowledge of computers, word processors, spreadsheets, and databases is important.

Most agencies that hire crime analysts require that applicants have a bachelor's degree. Many crime analysts have degrees in criminal justice, statistics, computer science, and sociology.

Outlook

As the job of the crime analyst becomes increasingly well known and as analysts' work continues to contribute to positive results for law enforcement agencies, the need for these professionals should grow. The emergence of community-oriented policing is one factor that has added to the need for crime analysts. This type of policing is intended to get police officers out on the streets of their communities rather than doing paperwork at a desk. To do this, many agencies are hiring civilians for desk jobs, which allow more police officers to have a presence in their community.

For More Information

There are many ways to begin your own training and education now. First of all, get some exposure to the law enforcement community by volunteering at the local police department. You can also join a program that offers a mini-course on law enforcement. Visit the National Institute of Justice Publications at http://www.asc14.com/JustPub.html for journals and other information published about crime.

American Academy of Forensic Sciences
PO Box 669
Colorado Springs, CO 80901-0669
719-636-1100
http://www.aafs.org

American Society of Criminology
1314 Kinnear Road
Columbus, OH 43212-1156
http://www.asc41.com

International Association of Crime Analysts
9218 Metcalf Avenue, #364
Overland Park, KS 66212
800-609-3419
http://www.iaca.net

Society of Certified Criminal Analysts
73 Gordon Avenue
Lawrenceville, NJ 08648
http://www.certifiedanalysts.net

Critical Care Nurses

What Critical Care Nurses Do

Critical care nurses are specialized nurses who provide highly skilled direct patient care to critically ill patients who need intense medical treatment because they are at risk for life-threatening illnesses. Contrary to previously held beliefs that critical care nurses work only in intensive care units (ICUs) or cardiac care units (CCUs) of hospitals, today's critical care nurses work in emergency departments, post anesthesia recovery units, pediatric intensive care units, burn units, and neonatal intensive care units of medical facilities as well as in other units that treat critically ill patients.

Specific job responsibilities vary according to which department they work in, but in most cases critical care nurses are assigned to only one or two patients because critically ill patients' problems are complex and unstable, requiring constant care and monitoring. Some hospitals require nurses to work 12-hour shifts, so critical care nursing can be very intense and exhausting.

In many cases, critical care nurses face situations that require them to act immediately on the patients' behalf. Nurses must be patient advocates, making sure that the patients receive the best possible care while respecting their wishes. Nurses must also provide support and education to the patients and their families. Because of the seriousness of their loved one's illness, family members and friends may be difficult to deal with, and critical care nurses must display patience, understanding, and composure during these emotional times. They must be able to communicate with the family and explain medical terminology and procedures to the patient and family to help them understand what is being done and why.

Critical care nurses have to keep up with the latest medical technology and research as well as medical treatments and procedures. They learn to operate high-tech machines, and they are frequently tested on how to use and operate them.

SCHOOL SUBJECTS
Biology, Chemistry
MINIMUM EDUCATION LEVEL
Some postsecondary training
SALARY RANGE
$34,000 to $49,000 to $70,000
OUTLOOK
Faster than the average

OTHER ARTICLES TO READ
Advanced Practice Nurses
Clinical Nurse Specialists
Neonatal Nurses
Nurse Anesthetists
Nurse Practitioners
Nurses

Critical care nursing can be emotionally draining but also rewarding when patients get through their medical crises.

Education and Training

Science, math, and health classes will prepare you for any nursing career. Before you can become a critical care nurse, you must become a registered nurse. (See Nurses.) Usually nurses have some bedside nursing experience before entering the critical care nursing field. However, some hospitals are developing graduate internship and orientation programs that allow new graduates to enter this specialty.

Registered nurses, regardless of specialty, must be licensed in order to practice in all 50 states and the District of Columbia. Critical care nursing certification programs are available through the American Association of Critical-Care Nurses. Some institutions may require certification as a critical care nurse.

Outlook

Employment of all registered nurses is expected to grow faster than the average in

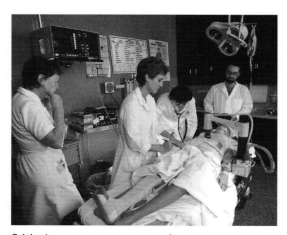

Critical care nurses treat a patient.

the next decade. Nursing specialties will be in great demand in the future, and a growing number of hospitals are experiencing a shortage of critical care nurses. Many hospitals that need critical care nurses are offering incentives such as sign-on bonuses. The greatest demand is for critical care nurses who specialize in a specific area of care, such as cardiovascular ICU, pediatric and neonatal ICU, and open-heart recovery units. Job opportunities vary across the country and are available in all geographic areas and in large and small hospitals.

For More Information

Visit nursing Web sites and read books and journals on careers in nursing. *The American Nurse* (http://www.nursingworld.org/tan) and *Nurse Week* (http://www.nurseweek.com) may be available at your public library.

American Association of Critical-Care Nurses
101 Columbia
Aliso Viejo, CA 92656-4109
info@aacn.org
http://www.aacn.org

American Nurses Association
600 Maryland Avenue, SW, Suite 100W
Washington, DC 20024-2571
http://www.nursingworld.org

Emergency Nurses Association
915 Lee Street
Des Plaines, IL 60016-6569
enainfo@ena.org
http://www.ena.org

National League for Nursing
61 Broadway
New York, NY 10006
nlnweb@nln.org
http://www.nln.org

Cruise Ship Workers

What Cruise Ship Workers Do

Cruise ship workers provide services to passengers on cruise ships. They assist in the operation of the ship, serve food and drink, and maintain cabins and public areas. Cruise ship workers also lead activities on the ship and provide entertainment. It takes hundreds and sometimes thousands of workers to make sure that the ship runs smoothly and all the passengers are comfortable. The crew is divided into six different departments. The captain, or the master of the ship, is in charge of the entire crew.

Deck. This department is responsible for the navigation of the ship. Workers oversee the maintenance of the hull and deck.

Engine. This staff operates and maintains machinery. Together, deck and engine staffs include officers, carpenters, seamen, maintenance workers, electricians, engineers, repairmen, plumbers, and incinerator operators.

Radio/broadcast department. *Videographers* are responsible for the maintenance and operation of the ship's broadcast booth. This includes radio and news telecasts. *Telephonists* help passengers place phone calls to people on shore.

Medical department. *Physicians* and *nurses* treat passengers whose illnesses range from seasickness to more serious health problems.

Steward. This department, one of the largest on board, is concerned with the comfort of all passengers. The food staff includes specially trained *chefs* that prepare meals. The *wait staff* serves guests in the formal dining room and provides room service. *Bartenders* mix and serve drinks at many stations throughout the ship. The housekeeping staff is composed of *room stewards* and *cleaners*, who keep cabins, public areas, and staterooms clean and orderly.

Pursers. This large department is responsible for guest relations and services. The *chief purser* is the main contact for passengers regarding the ship's policies

SCHOOL SUBJECTS
Foreign language, Geography, Speech

MINIMUM EDUCATION LEVEL
High school diploma

SALARY RANGE
$13,000 to $19,000 to $33,000

OUTLOOK
About as fast as the average

OTHER ARTICLES TO READ
Cooks, Chefs, and Bakers
Gaming Workers
Hotel and Motel Managers and Workers
Recreation Workers
Resort Workers
Ski Resort Workers

and procedures. *Assistant pursers* assist the chief with various duties. They provide guest services, ship information, monetary exchange, postage, safety deposit boxes, and other duties usually associated with the front desk department of a hotel. The cruise staff is headed by the *cruise director*. This staff plans daily activities and entertainment. The *youth staff* plans activities and games specifically designed for children. Ships with a casino on board employ casino workers, including game dealers, cashiers, keno runners, and slot machine attendants. Many *entertainers* and *musicians* are hired to sing, dance, and perform comedy skits and musical shows. *Dance instructors* teach dance classes ranging from ballroom to country line dances.

Education and Training

Cruise lines require at least a high school diploma, or the equivalent, for most entry-level jobs.

For a job with more responsibility, such as an officer-level job, you'll need a college degree as well as past work experience. Many employees, especially those in the cruise staff, have an entertainment background. Youth staff members usually have a background in education or recreation.

Some technical positions, such as engine room workers, require certification. Nurses and physicians must be licensed to practice medicine.

Outlook

Overall, the cruise line industry is still one of the fastest growing segments of the travel industry. Job growth for cruise ship workers should continue to be strong through 2012.

Cruise ship workers must attend to cruise passengers' needs.

For More Information

To learn more about the work of a cruise ship worker, interview a cruise ship worker, if possible, or speak to people that have gone on cruises.

Cruise Lines International Association
500 Fifth Avenue, Suite 1407
New York, NY 10110
http://www.cruising.org

Cruise Services International
601 Dundas Street West
Box 24070
Whitby, ON L1N 8X8 Canada
http://www.cruisedreamjob.com

Cryptographic Technicians

SKILLS SPOTLIGHT
♦
What they do
Evaluate and manage information
Help clients and customers
Select and apply tools/technology

Skills they need
Integrity/honesty
Mathematics
Problem solving

What Cryptographic Technicians Do

Cryptographic technicians operate equipment used for coding, decoding, and sending secret messages. They are employed by the government in all branches of the military. They are also employed by government agencies such as the National Security Agency, the Federal Bureau of Intelligence, the Department of State, and other intelligence operations. Cryptographic technicians work for industries that do private business through the computer, such as the banking industry.

In order to code and send secret messages, cryptographic technicians first select the particular code that they should use for the message. Then they set up their machine to translate the message into that code, and they type the message into the machine. The machine converts the message into code form in a process known as encryption. After the message is encrypted, the technicians send the message to a receiver via telephone lines, satellites, or other kinds of communication links.

When receiving a coded message, cryptographic technicians feed the incoming transmission into a decoding machine and take the resulting message to its intended receiver. If a message appears to have been coded incorrectly, technicians may try to straighten out the message using special decoding procedures and equipment, or they may request that the message be sent again. In sending and receiving coded messages, cryptographic technicians may operate teletype machines or radio transmitters and receivers.

The banking industry, or any other industry requiring computer security, must prevent unauthorized access in order to protect the accounts or data in their files. For instance, a message to transfer money from one bank to another is sometimes sent by computer. To prevent transfers from being done by someone who is not

SCHOOL SUBJECTS
English, Mathematics

MINIMUM EDUCATION LEVEL
Bachelor's degree

SALARY RANGE
$25,000 to $38,000 to $69,000

OUTLOOK
About as fast as the average

OTHER ARTICLES TO READ
Computer Programmers
Computer Security Specialists
Detectives
FBI Agents
Military Workers
Police Officers
Spies

authorized to do them, the banks send the message in code.

In the U.S. Armed Forces, cryptographic technicians play an important role in our military success. When military workers are on a training mission abroad or at war, they rely on coded messages sent by cryptographic technicians for updates on world events and transmission of orders from their superiors.

Education and Training

In high school, you should take courses in mathematics and English. Computer science, foreign language, and business classes will also be helpful.

Cryptographic technicians must be high school graduates, although more and more private companies and military positions are requiring two to four years of college education. Positions with federal intelligence and investigative agencies, such as the Federal Bureau of Investigation and the Central Intelligence Agency, generally require at least a bachelor's degree and/or several years of related experience. Prospective cryptographic technicians need to receive special training that lasts from six months to a year. The U.S. Armed Forces and government agencies that hire cryptographic technicians will usually provide this training.

Due to the secret nature of their work, applicants often must undergo a thorough character investigation, and their records for the past 10 years are checked.

Outlook

The need for skilled cryptographic technicians should remain high as normal U.S. intelligence operations take place throughout the world and as the government works to address new terrorist threats. Hackers, people who illegally break into private and public computer systems, have become increasingly talented at getting past even the tightest security programs. Companies will most likely hire more cryptographic technicians to prevent these computer break-ins.

For More Information

Enlisting in a branch of the Armed Forces or joining the Reserve Officers Training Corps after high school is a good way to start a career in cryptology. You may also want to subscribe to the *Journal of Cryptology* to learn more about this field.

American Cryptogram Association
PO Box 1013
Londonderry, NH 03053-1013
http://www.cryptogram.org

Cryptography Research Inc.
575 Market Street, 21st Floor
San Francisco, CA 94105
http://www.cryptography.com

International Association for Cryptographic Research
PO Box 791
Palo Alto, CA 94301
http://www.iacr.org

A National Security Agency employee works a cryptologic problem using an overhead projector.

Cultural Advisers

What Cultural Advisers Do

The world is becoming a smaller place—not in terms of actual size, but in our ability to communicate and do business with people from far-away countries. Companies, organizations, and educational institutions in the United States need to be able to communicate with all branches of their organization, which may be located in foreign countries such as Russia, Japan, or Kenya. People in other countries may not be comfortable speaking English, eating the types of food that Americans like to eat, or even saying hello and goodbye the same way. This is why businesses need experts to help smooth over these cultural differences.

Cultural advisers work to bridge gaps in communication and culture. They are also known as *bilingual consultants*. They are fluent in two languages and two cultures. Besides their bilingual skills, these advisers are usually experts in another area. For example, a banking and finance expert who speaks Japanese and has traveled to Japan would have the necessary background to become a cultural adviser for an American steel company looking to do business in Japan.

Cultural advisers help their clients learn what they can do better when dealing with other cultures and countries. They also help to identify which business practices or social rules need improvement. Cultural advisers may work for a consulting agency or be self-employed. Some advisers work on judging written communication and marketing materials. Others may offer advice on business practices.

The area that cultural advisers work in depends on their specialty. Some specialties include management, finance, banking, education, law, marketing, human resources, and computer technology.

Cultural advisers travel often. Projects may be demanding at times, and advisers may have to work many more hours than the typical workweek.

Education and Training

If you are interested in a career as a cultural adviser, concentrate on languages and the

SCHOOL SUBJECTS
Foreign language, Geography, Speech

MINIMUM EDUCATION LEVEL
Bachelor's degree

SALARY RANGE
$14,000 to $48,000 to $83,000

OUTLOOK
Faster than the average

OTHER ARTICLES TO READ
Business Managers
Internet Executives
Interpreters and Translators
Management Analysts and Consultants
Purchasing Agents

social sciences in high school. It is important that you learn another language and become familiar with the cultures of the countries where that language is spoken. Social sciences, such as geography, history, and sociology, will help to give you a broader world view.

In college, you should continue language and social science courses. You will also need to take classes in an area of specialization, such as business, education, or law. Taking business classes in college will also help your chances of becoming an independent adviser and business owner. If you have the opportunity to study or live abroad, that experience will also be helpful.

A cultural adviser translates a conversation between a French businessman and an American businessman.

Outlook

It is expected that the field of cultural advising will grow faster than the average in the next decade. More cultural advisors will be needed as trade with other countries becomes easier and U.S. companies do more business around the world. Latin America and Asia are two promising areas for American businesses.

Cultural advisers will also be needed to support and assist the increasingly diverse population within the United States. Competition is keen, however, and those with graduate degrees and specific expertise will be the most successful.

For More Information

If you are interested in a career as a cultural adviser, a good way to explore this field is to join one of your high school's foreign language clubs. In addition to using the foreign language, these clubs often have activities related to the culture where the language is spoken. Learn as much as you can about people and life in other parts of the world. You will also gain valuable experience through study and living abroad programs that you can apply to even while in high school.

Association of Career Firms International
204 E Street, NE
Washington, DC 20002
202-547-6344
aocfi@aocfi.org
http://www.aocfi.org

Rotary International
One Rotary Center
1560 Sherman Avenue
Evanston, IL 60201
847-866-3000
http://www.rotary.org

Customer Service Representatives

SKILLS SPOTLIGHT

◆

What they do
Evaluate and manage information
Help clients and customers
Work with a team

Skills they need
Social
Speaking/listening
Responsibility

What Customer Service Representatives Do

Customer service representatives work with customers to assist with problems and answer questions. Customer service representatives work in many different industries to provide "front-line" customer service. Most customer service representatives work in an office setting, although some may work in the field to better meet customer needs.

Customer service representatives often handle complaints and problems. They should be pleasant and efficient while dealing with customers, no matter how upset the customer may be.

Many customer service representatives answer calls that come in on toll-free telephone lines. While some calls are likely to be focused on complaints or questions, some are simpler. Some people call to order literature or brochures or to find their nearest dealer location.

Customer service representatives work in a variety of fields and businesses, but they all have one thing in common: the customer. All companies must depend on their customers to keep them in business. Therefore, customer service, whether handled by the company itself or by another company, is extremely important.

Some customer service representatives do the majority of their work on the telephone. Others represent companies in the field, where the customer actually uses the product or service. Still other customer service representatives may specialize in helping customers over the Internet.

Some companies have customer service representatives available 24 hours a day and seven days a week, so a variety of shifts are required. Not all customer service representatives work a varied schedule, though. Many work traditional daytime hours.

A successful customer service representative will most likely have an outgoing personality and enjoy working with people and assisting them with their questions and problems.

SCHOOL SUBJECTS
Business, English, Speech

MINIMUM EDUCATION LEVEL
High school diploma

SALARY RANGE
$17,000 to $26,000 to $43,000

OUTLOOK
Faster than the average

OTHER ARTICLES TO READ
Business Managers
Labor Union Business Agents
Management Analysts and Consultants
Secretaries
Technical Support Specialists

This customer service representative fields calls from customers with questions or concerns about her company's product.

Education and Training

If you are interested in becoming a customer service representative, take classes that focus on communication and business in high school. English and speech classes will help with all forms of communication. Business classes will give an overview of the business world and how customer service fits into that world. A high school diploma is required for most customer service representative positions.

A college degree is not required to become a customer service representative. However, any postsecondary education at a college or other training program will help you advance in your career as a customer service representative.

Outlook

Employment for customer service representatives should grow faster than the average through 2012. This is a large field of workers. Many replacement workers are needed each year as representatives leave this job for other positions, retire, or leave for other reasons. In addition, the Internet and e-commerce should increase the demand for customer service representatives who will be needed to help customers navigate Web sites, answer questions over the phone, and respond to e-mails.

For More Information

To learn more about a career as a customer service representative, get a part-time job that involves dealing with customers on an everyday basis. Volunteer to answer phones at a local business. It will also be helpful to interview someone who works with customers every day so you can get an idea of what types of advantages and disadvantages the job has to offer.

The Association of Support Professionals
66 Mt. Auburn Street
Watertown, MA 02472-3929
617-924-3944, ext. 14
http://www.asponline.com

Customer Care Institute
17 Dean Overlook, NW
Atlanta, GA 30318
404-352-9291
http://www.customercare.com

Help Desk Institute
6385 Corporate Drive, Suite 301
Colorado Springs, CO 80919
800-248-0174
http://www.helpdeskinst.com

International Customer Service Association
401 North Michigan Avenue, Suite 2200
Chicago, IL 60611-4267
800-360-4272
http://www.icsa.com

Customs Officials

What Customs Officials Do

Customs officials make sure illegal merchandise, known as contraband, is not smuggled into the United States. Drugs are an example of the contraband that these officials look for. Customs officials are employed by the federal government to enforce the laws that limit which goods can come into the country (imports) and which goods leave the country (exports). Customs officials work at airports, seaports, and border crossings at every entry and exit point of the United States.

Customs officials need to be observant and crafty to search out all the possible hiding places in luggage or clothes where people might hide contraband. Federal law prevents other items besides drugs from being transported across borders, including certain plants and foods that could carry insects and disease. Importing many species of animals, and products made from them, is also against the law.

At airports and seaports, customs officials check the luggage and personal items of airline and ship passengers and crew members. These travelers and workers must tell customs officials exactly what goods they have with them. This procedure is also called declaring merchandise. Customs officials also check the goods that the ship or airplane is carrying. They make sure that all merchandise is declared honestly, that taxes are paid, and that no contraband is present. Customs officials also determine taxes, called duties, that people must pay on imports and exports.

Travelers sometimes try to hide expensive imports to avoid paying high duties on them. Customs officials need to be as alert to these tax evaders (people trying to avoid paying taxes) as they are to drug dealers. At border-crossing points, customs officials check the baggage of travelers who come by car or train to and from Canada and Mexico.

The United States imports many products, which are then sold or used for industry. Customs officials examine, count, weigh, gauge, measure, and sample commercial

SCHOOL SUBJECTS
English, Government

MINIMUM EDUCATION LEVEL
High school diploma

SALARY RANGE
$25,000 to $42,000 to $65,000

OUTLOOK
Faster than the average

OTHER ARTICLES TO READ
Border Patrol Officers
Deputy U.S. Marshals
FBI Agents
Forensic Experts
Health and Regulatory Inspectors
Police Officers

goods. They try to determine how much goods are worth by referring to shipping papers. Customs officials then figure how much import tax should be paid.

Education and Training

To be a customs worker, you must be a U.S. citizen and at least 21 years old. You'll need a minimum of a high school diploma, but a college degree is preferred.

In high school, take courses in government, geography, social studies, English, history, and physical education. Foreign language classes will be helpful as well. If you'd like to become a specialist in the scientific or investigative aspects of the U.S. Customs Service, you'll need to take science classes, such as chemistry, and computer science.

Without a college degree, you must have at least three years of general work experience involving contact with the public. Customs inspectors, like all employees of the federal government, must pass a physical examination and undergo a security check. You must also pass a standardized test called the Professional and Administrative Career Examination.

Outlook

Following the terrorist acts of September 11, 2001, national attention was drawn to the need for more security measures to be taken at U.S. borders, in U.S. airports, and in dealing with travelers throughout the United States. This higher security should result in an increased need for all law enforcement officers, including customs officials. It is predicted that employment for police and detectives, a category including customs officials, will grow faster than the average through 2012.

A U.S. Customs Inspector checks seaport containers coming into the United States as they are unloaded from a ship at the Port of Miami.

For More Information

To learn more about this profession, talk with people employed as customs inspectors, or contact local labor union organizations. The U.S. Customs Service has an Explorer program that can give you the opportunity to experience law-enforcement activities related to Customs Service careers.

Immigration and Naturalization Service
INS Office of Business Liaison
425 I Street, NW, Room 3034
Washington, DC 20536
http://www.uscis.gov

U.S. Customs Service
1300 Pennsylvania Avenue, NW
Washington, DC 20229
http://www.cbp.gov

Cytotechnologists

What Cytotechnologists Do

Cytotechnologists are laboratory specialists who study cells under microscopes, searching for cell abnormalities such as changes in color, shape, or size that might indicate the presence of disease. Cytotechnologists may also assist physicians in the collection of body cells from various body sites, prepare slides, keep records, file reports, and consult with coworkers and pathologists.

Cytotechnologists primarily examine prepared slides of body cells by viewing them through a microscope. In any single slide, there may be more than 100,000 cells, so it is important that cytotechnologists be patient, thorough, and accurate when performing their job. They are required to study the slides and examine cell growth patterns, looking for abnormal patterns or changes in a cell's color, shape, or size that might indicate the presence of disease.

While most cytotechnologists spend the majority of their workday in the laboratory, some might assist doctors at patients' bedsides collecting cell samples from the respiratory and urinary systems, as well as the gastrointestinal tract. They might also assist physicians with bronchoscopes and with needle aspirations, a process that uses very fine needles to suction cells from many locations within the body. Once the cells are collected, cytotechnologists may prepare the slides for microscope examination. In some laboratories, cell preparation is done by medical technicians known as *cytotechnicians*.

Although they usually work independently in the lab, they often share lab space and must consult with co-workers, supervisors, and pathologists regarding their findings. Most cytotechnologists work for private firms that are hired by physicians to evaluate medical tests, but they may also work for hospitals or university research institutions.

Education and Training

Biology, chemistry, and other science courses are essential if you want to become a cytotechnologist. In addition, math, English, and computer literacy classes are also important.

SCHOOL SUBJECTS
Biology, Chemistry

MINIMUM EDUCATION LEVEL
Bachelor's degree

SALARY RANGE
$31,000 to $44,000 to $61,000

OUTLOOK
About as fast as the average

OTHER ARTICLES TO READ
Biologists
Biomedical Equipment Technicians
Physician Assistants
Physicians
X-ray Technologists

There are two options for becoming a cytotechnologist. The first involves earning a bachelor's degree in biology, life sciences, or a related field, and then entering a one-year, postgraduate certificate program offered by an accredited hospital or university.

The second option involves transferring into a cytotechnology program during your junior or senior year of college. Students on this track earn a bachelor of science degree in cytotechnology. In both cases, you would earn a college degree and complete at least one year of training devoted to cytotechnology. The courses you will take include chemistry, biology, business, and math.

Cytotechnology graduates (from either degree programs or certificate programs) may register for the certification examination given by the Board of Registry of the American Society of Clinical Pathologists. Most employers require that new employees be certified.

Outlook

Employment of cytotechnologists is expected to grow as fast as the average for all occupations through 2012. The job outlook for cytotechnologists should remain healthy over the next decade, as the volume of laboratory tests increases with population growth and the development of new types of tests.

For More Information

Participate in science clubs and competitions that help you become more familiar with microscopes and allow you to practice slides. Ask a science teacher, counselor, or parent to contact museums involved

Cytotechnologists examine cells under microscopes to find signs of cancer or other illnesses.

in research to request viewing their slide collections and slide preparation process.

American Society for Cytotechnology
1500 Sunday Drive, Suite 102
Raleigh, NC 27607
800-948-3947
info@asct.com
http://www.asct.com

American Society of Clinical Pathology
2100 West Harrison Street
Chicago, IL 60612
312-738-1336
info@ascp.org
http://www.ascp.org

American Society of Cytopathology
400 West 9th Street, Suite 201
Wilmington, DE 19801
302-429-8802
http://www.cytopathology.org

Dancers

What Dancers Do

Dancers use body movements to tell a story, express an idea or feeling, or entertain their audiences. Professional dancers often belong to a dance company, a group of dancers that work together on a repertoire, which is a collection of dances they perform regularly.

Most dancers study some ballet or classical dance. Classical dance training gives dancers a good foundation for most other types of dance. Traditionally, ballets tell stories, although today's ballets express a variety of themes and ideas.

Modern dance developed early in the 20th century, and it got its roots from classical ballet. Jazz dance is a form of modern dance often seen in Broadway productions. Tap dance combines sound and movement. Tap dancers tap out rhythms with metal cleats that are attached to the toes and heels of their shoes. Other dance forms include ballroom dance, folk or ethnic dance, and acrobatic dance.

Dancers may perform in classical ballets, musical stage shows, folk dance shows, television shows, films, or music videos.

Because dancing jobs are not always available, many dancers work as part-time dance instructors. Dancers who create new dance routines are called *choreographers*. (See Choreographers.)

Dancers begin training early and have fairly short careers. Most professional ballet and modern dancers retire by age 40 because dancing becomes too physically demanding for their bodies. They become dance teachers, artistic directors, or choreographers, or they start other careers.

The physical demands of daily practice as well as the demands of the dance routine necessitate good health and a strong body. A dancer must also have a feeling for music, a sense of rhythm, and grace and agility.

Education and Training

Dancers usually begin training around the age of 10, or sometimes even as early as age seven or eight. They may study with private

SCHOOL SUBJECTS
Music, Physical education, Theater/dance

MINIMUM EDUCATION LEVEL
High school diploma

SALARY RANGE
$13,000 to $21,000 to $53,000

OUTLOOK
About as fast as the average

OTHER ARTICLES TO READ
Actors
Choreographers
Circus Performers
Musicians
Professional Athletes—Individual Sports
Professional Athletes—Team Sports

teachers or in ballet schools. Dancers who are especially good in their early teens may receive professional training in a regional ballet school or a major ballet company. By the age of 17 or 18, dancers begin to audition for positions in professional dance companies.

If you are interested in a career as a dancer, take theater/dance, physical education, art, and drama classes in high school.

Many colleges and universities offer degrees in dance. Those who teach dance in a college or university often are required to have a degree. Also, since the professional life of a dancer can be rather short, a college degree will give you better options for a second career after retiring from dance performance.

Dancers devote many hours to routines to achieve the effect of effortless perfection during performance.

Outlook

Employment of dancers is expected to increase about as fast as the national average through the next decade. Those seeking a career in dancing will find that the field is highly competitive and uncertain. For performers, opportunities are limited, since there are more trained dancers than job openings. Television has provided additional positions for dancers, but the number of stage and screen productions is declining.

Although all dancers are different, the average chorus dancer can expect a career that lasts five to 10 years at the most. A dancer who can move from performing to teaching will find other employment possibilities in colleges, universities, and schools of dance. It is also possible to find employment with civic and community groups, or by operating a dance studio.

For More Information

To prepare for a career as a dancer, take as many dance classes as you can. Once you have learned some dance technique, begin to give recitals and performances for family and friends. Audition for school or community stage productions that have dance numbers.

Dance Magazine
111 Myrtle Street, Suite 203
Oakland, CA 94607
510-839-6060
dancemag@dancemagazine.com
http://www.dancemagazine.com

Dance/USA
1156 15th Street, NW, Suite 820
Washington, DC 20005-1726
danceusa@danceusa.org
http://www.danceusa.org

National Dance Association
1900 Association Drive
Reston, VA 20191-1598
800-213-7193 ext. 464
nda@aahperd.org
http://www.aahperd.org/nda

Database Specialists

SKILLS SPOTLIGHT
◆
What they do
Create or improve systems
Evaluate and manage information
Select and apply tools/technology

Skills they need
Decision making
Mathematics
Problem solving

What Database Specialists Do

A collection of information stored in a computer is called a database. *Database specialists* work for utility companies, stores, investment companies, insurance companies, publishing firms, telecommunications firms, and all branches of government. They set up and maintain databases. They purchase computer equipment and create computer programs that collect, analyze, store, and send information.

Database specialists figure out the type of computer system that the company needs. They meet with top-level company officials to discuss these needs. Together they decide what type of hardware and software will be required to set up a certain type of database. Then a database design analyst writes a proposal that states the company's needs, the type of equipment that will meet those needs, and how much this equipment will cost.

Database specialists set up the computer system that the company buys. *Database managers* and *database administrators* decide how to organize and store the information in the database. They create a computer program or a series of programs and train employees to enter information into computers.

Computer programs sometimes crash, or stop working properly. Database specialists make sure that a backup copy of the program and the database is available in case a crash occurs. Specialists are also responsible for making sure that the database is protected from people or organizations who are not supposed to see it. A company's database contains important, and sometimes secret, information.

Large companies may have many databases. Sometimes it is necessary for these databases to share information. Database managers see to it that these different databases can communicate with each other, even if they are located in different parts of the country.

SCHOOL SUBJECTS
Chemistry, Computer science, Mathematics

MINIMUM EDUCATION LEVEL
Associate's degree

SALARY RANGE
$32,000 to $59,000 to $96,000

OUTLOOK
Much faster than the average

OTHER ARTICLES TO READ
Computer Programmers
Computer Trainers
Computer-Aided Design Technicians
Graphic Designers
Hardware Engineers
Software Designers
Software Engineers

Consulting recent publications, a database manager updates a computer file used by clients for information services.

Education and Training

To prepare for a career as a database specialist, take as many computer courses as possible. In addition, you should study mathematics, accounting, science, English, and communications in high school.

You'll need a minimum of an associate's degree in a computer-related technology for entry-level database positions. A bachelor's degree in computer science or business administration is necessary for advanced positions. A master's degree in this field will provide you with even greater opportunities.

Some database specialists become certified for jobs in the computer field by passing an examination given by the Institute for Certification of Computing Professionals (http://www.iccp.org).

Outlook

The use of computers and database systems in almost all business settings creates a number of opportunities for well-qualified database workers. Database specialists and computer support specialists are predicted to be among the fastest growing occupations through 2012.

Employment opportunities for database specialists will be best in large urban areas, since there are so many businesses and organizations located there that need employees to work with their databases. Since smaller communities are also rapidly developing significant job opportunities, skilled workers can pick from a wide range of jobs throughout the country. Those with the best education and the most experience in computer systems and personnel management will have the best job opportunities.

For More Information

School computer clubs are a good way to learn about computers and meet others who are interested in the field. There are also training programs, such as those offered at summer camps and community centers, that teach computer literacy. Volunteer to work on databases at your school, religious institution, or local charity.

Association for Women in Computing
41 Sutter Street, Suite 1006
San Francisco, California 94104 USA
info@awc-hq.org
http://www.awc-hq.org

Association of Information Technology Professionals
33405 Treasury Center
Chicago, IL 60694-3400
aitp_hq@aitp.org
http://www.aitp.org

Data Entry Clerks

SKILLS SPOTLIGHT
◆
What they do
Evaluate and manage information
Manage time
Select and apply tools/technology

Skills they need
Mathematics
Reading/writing
Self-management

What Data Entry Clerks Do

Data entry clerks transfer information from paper documents to a computer system. The information can be processed at various times to produce important business documents such as sales reports, billing invoices, mailing lists, and many other documents.

From a source document such as a financial statement, data entry clerks type in information in either alphabetic, numeric, or symbolic code. The information is entered using a keyboard, either the regular typewriter-like computer keyboard or a more customized keypad developed for a certain industry or business. The entry machine converts the coded information into either electronic impulses or a series of holes in a tape that the computer can read and process electronically. Newer, more sophisticated computers have eliminated the need for magnetic tapes and rely exclusively on word processing or spreadsheet data files. Some data entry work involves entering special instructions that tell the computer what functions to perform and when.

Accuracy is an essential element of all data entry work. Data entry clerks must consistently check their computer screens for obvious errors and systematically refer back to the source documents to ensure that they entered the information correctly. Sometimes *verifier operators* are employed specifically to perform accuracy tests of previously processed information.

Data-coder operators examine the information in the source material to determine what codes and symbols should be used to enter it into the computer. They may write the operating instructions for the data entry staff and assist the system programmer in testing and revising computer programs designed to process data entry work.

Terminal operators also use coding systems to input information from the source document into a series of alphabetic or numeric signals that can be read by the computer. After checking their work for accuracy, they send the data to the computer system via telephone lines or other

---

SCHOOL SUBJECTS
Business, Computer science, English

MINIMUM EDUCATION LEVEL
High school diploma

SALARY RANGE
$16,000 to $23,000 to $34,000

OUTLOOK
Decline

OTHER ARTICLES TO READ
Clerks
Computer and Office Machine Technicians
Database Specialists
Secretaries

remote-transmission methods if they do not input directly into the computer network.

Education and Training

In high school, you should take English, typing, computer science, and other business courses that focus on the operation of office machinery. A high school diploma is usually required for data entry work. In a growing number of cases, some college or technical school training is desirable. Most data entry clerks receive on-the-job training pertaining specifically to the computer system and input procedures used by the employer.

Most companies test prospective employees to evaluate their typing skills in terms of both speed and accuracy. Competency in general mathematics and spelling is frequently reviewed as well. As computers continue to change, you must always be ready to learn new methods and techniques of input.

Outlook

Because of improvements in data-processing technology that enable businesses to process greater volumes of information with fewer workers, the U.S. Department of Labor predicts that the employment outlook for data entry clerks is expected to decline through 2012. Jobs are becoming limited, for example, because many computer systems can now send information directly to another computer system without the need for a data entry clerk to input the information a second time. In addition, the widespread use of personal computers, which

A data entry clerk busily enters information into a database.

permit numerous employees to enter data directly, have also diminished the need for skilled entry personnel. More businesses are also contracting temporary and staffing services instead of hiring full-time data entry clerks.

For More Information

A visit to an office that uses data processing systems may provide a good opportunity to learn more about this position. At home or school, you can practice typing by using a computer or typewriter or by entering data for various club or group activities.

Association for Computing Machinery
One Astor Plaza
1515 Broadway, 17th Floor
New York, NY 10036-5701
212-869-7440
http://www.acm.org

Association of Information Technology Professionals
401 North Michigan Avenue, Suite 2200
Chicago, IL 60611-4267
800-224-9371
http://www.aitp.org

 Demographers

What Demographers Do

Demographers collect and study facts about population. They gather information about births, marriages, deaths, education, and income levels. Their population studies tell what the society is actually like and help experts predict economic and social trends.

For example, demographers may study birth rates of a community. They may find that the population of school-age children is growing faster than expected and that new schools will have to be built. Or demographers may collect facts about how many of these children have been sick with measles. These facts could be studied to find out how effective the measles vaccine is.

Demographers work for both government agencies and private companies. Local, state, and federal government agencies use demographers to help them provide enough of the right kinds of transportation, education, police, and health services. Private companies use demographers' collections of facts, or statistics, to help them improve their products or services and know who will buy them. For example, a retail chain might use a demographer's statistics to help decide the best location to open a new store. Demographers may also teach in colleges and universities or work as consultants for private companies or communities as a whole.

An *applied statistician,* a specialized type of demographer, uses accepted theories and known statistical formulas to collect and analyze data in a specific area, such as the availability of health care in a specified location.

Demographers use computers to help them gather and analyze the millions of pieces of information they need to base their predictions on. Demographers must know how to read the statistics and put them together in a meaningful way.

Education and Training

If you are interested in a career as a demographer, you should be good at solving logical problems and have strong skills in mathematics, especially algebra and geometry. In high school, take classes in social studies, English, and mathematics. Familiarity with computer database programs is important.

Demographers must have a bachelor's degree in sociology or public health with special studies in demography. Many entry-level jobs require a master's degree as well.

As this field gets more competitive, many demographers (especially those who wish to work for the federal government) will earn a doctoral degree in sociology. The most successful demographers specialize in one area. You must also keep up with advances in the field by continuing education throughout your career.

Outlook

The social science field is expected to grow about as fast as the average through 2012. However, there will be keen competition in many areas. Those with the most training and greatest amount of education, preferably a Ph.D., should find the best job prospects. Employment opportunities should be greatest in and around large metropolitan areas, where many colleges, universities, and other research facilities are located, as well as at federal agencies. Those with statistical training will have an advantage, and those with advanced degrees will be preferred by private industry.

For More Information

Exploring statistical surveys and information from the Gallup Organization (http://www.gallup.com) is another way to gather information. Additionally, undertaking your own demographic survey of an organization or group, such as your school or after-school club, is a project you may want to try.

A demographer maps population trends on a computer.

American Sociological Association
1307 New York Avenue, NW, Suite 700
Washington, DC 20005
executive.office@asanet.org
http://www.asanet.org

Population Reference Bureau
1875 Connecticut Avenue, NW, Suite 520
Washington, DC 20009-5728
popref@prb.org
http://www.prb.org

Society for Applied Sociology
2342 Shattuck Avenue #362
Berkeley, CA 94704
510-548-6174
http://www.appliedsoc.org

U.S. Census Bureau
4700 Silver Hill Road
Washington, DC 20233
recruiter@census.gov
http://www.census.gov

# Dental Assistants

What Dental Assistants Do

Dental assistants help dentists examine and treat patients. They also carry out administrative tasks that make the dentist's office run smoothly.

Dental assistants greet patients and take them to the examining room. They prepare patients for examination by covering their clothing with paper or cloth to protect it from water and stains. They also adjust the chair and its headrest to the proper height.

Many dental assistants take X rays of patients' teeth and develop the film for the dentist. During examinations and dental procedures, dental assistants hand instruments to the dentist as they are needed. They also use suction devices to keep the patient's mouth dry. When the examination or procedure is over, dental assistants give patients instructions for taking care of their teeth and keeping their mouths clean and healthy.

Dental assistants help with a variety of other tasks, such as making plaster casts of a patient's teeth or making dentures. In some cases, they apply medications to teeth and gums or remove excess material after cavities have been filled. Dental assistants also may help dentists with any emergencies that arise during dental procedures.

In addition to assisting with dental procedures, many office tasks are performed by dental assistants. They keep patient records, answer telephones, schedule appointments, prepare bills, collect payments, and issue receipts. They may also inventory dental supplies.

Dental assistants are not the same as dental hygienists, who are licensed to clean and polish teeth.

Education and Training

If you are interested in a career as a dental assistant, prepare by taking courses in general science, biology, health, chemistry, and business management in high school. Typing is also important for dental assistants.

Many dental assistant positions require little or no experience and no education

---

SCHOOL SUBJECTS
Biology, Business, Health

MINIMUM EDUCATION LEVEL
High school diploma

SALARY RANGE
$19,000 to $28,000 to $41,000

OUTLOOK
Much faster than the average

OTHER ARTICLES TO READ
Dental Hygienists
Dental Laboratory Technicians
Endodontists
Nurse Assistants
Orthodontists

---

beyond high school. You will learn skills on the job. However, some assistants receive training after high school at a technical institute or a community or junior college that offers dental assisting programs. If you attend a two-year college program, you'll receive an associate's degree. If you attend technical school, you finish after one year and earn a certificate or diploma. To enter these programs, candidates must have a high school diploma, and some schools require that applicants have received good grades in science, typing, and English. Aspiring dental assistants can also receive training in the United States military.

Outlook

Employment for dental assistants is expected to grow much faster than the average through 2012. The average age of our population as a whole is rising, and people are becoming more aware that they can keep all their teeth and be healthy. Because of this, more people will seek dental services for cosmetic improvements and to keep their teeth healthy.

For More Information

To learn more about a career as a dental assistant, observe and interview a local dental assistant. It will also be helpful to get a part-time or summer job doing clerical work at a dentist's office.

American Dental Assistants Association
203 North LaSalle Street, Suite 1320
Chicago, IL 60601-1225
312-541-1550
adaa1@aol.com
http://www.dentalassistant.org

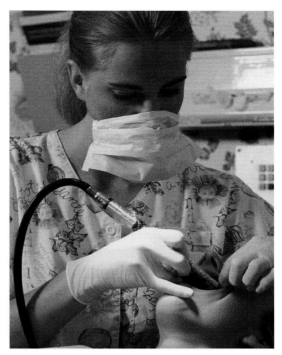

A dental assistant removes plaque from a patient's teeth during an exam.

American Dental Association
211 East Chicago Avenue
Chicago, IL 60611
312-440-2500
publicinfo@ada.org
http://www.ada.org

American Dental Education Association
1625 Massachusetts Avenue, NW, Suite 600
Washington, DC 20036-2212
202-667-9433
adea@adea.org
http://www.adea.org

Dental Assisting National Board
676 North Saint Clair, Suite 1880
Chicago, IL 60611
800-367-3262
danbmail@dentalassisting.com
http://www.dentalassisting.com

Dental Hygienists

What Dental Hygienists Do

Dental hygienists are licensed to clean patients' teeth and they usually work with dentists. Their main job is to remove plaque and other deposits from teeth polish teeth, and massage gums. Dental hygienists also teach good oral health. They show patients how to select toothbrushes and use floss. They also teach patients about which kinds of foods damage teeth and which habits, such as smoking, have harmful effects on teeth. The main goal of a dental hygienist is to help patients prevent tooth and gum decay and have a healthy mouth.

Hygienists who work for dentists in private practice may do more than clean teeth. They may take and develop X rays, mix materials to fill cavities, assist in surgery, and keep charts of patients' teeth. Hygienists may also sterilize (clean to get rid of all bacteria) instruments. Some hygienists have office duties as well, such as answering phone calls and scheduling appointments for patients.

Not all hygienists work for dentists. Some work in schools, where they clean and examine students' teeth and show them how to prevent tooth decay. They teach children and teens how to brush and floss teeth correctly and eat the right foods. Hygienists also keep records of the students' teeth and tell parents about any problems or need for more treatment.

Some dental hygienists work for local, state, or federal public health agencies. They clean the teeth of adults and children in public health clinics and other public facilities, and educate patients in the proper care of teeth.

Education and Training

To become a dental hygienist, you must have a high school diploma. It is a good idea to take classes such as biology, business, chemistry, English, health, and mathematics in high school.

You must also complete two or four years of college at an accredited dental hy-

SCHOOL SUBJECTS
Biology, Health

MINIMUM EDUCATION LEVEL
Associate's degree

SALARY RANGE
$36,000 to $57,000 to $84,000

OUTLOOK
Much faster than the average

OTHER ARTICLES TO READ
Dental Assistants
Dental Laboratory Technicians
Dentists
Endodontists
Medical Assistants
Orthodontists

giene school and pass the national board exams for your state. There are two types of dental hygiene programs. One is a four-year college program offering a bachelor's degree. The other is a two-year program leading to a dental hygiene certification. Many employers now require the four-year degree. During your education, you will study anatomy, physiology, chemistry, pharmacology, nutrition, and other sciences. You will also learn to handle delicate instruments, gain experience in the dental laboratory, and practice working with patients in clinics.

Dental hygienists, after graduation from accredited schools, must pass state licensing examinations, both written and clinical.

Outlook

It is predicted that employment of dental hygienists will grow much faster than the average through 2012. The demand for hygienists is expected to grow because younger generations that grew up receiving solid dental care will keep their healthy teeth for years longer than people have in the past. The fact that many people have dental insurance available to them will make dental work more affordable. As the population ages, there will be a special demand for hygienists to work with older people, especially those who live in nursing homes.

For More Information

To learn more about this field, ask your dental hygienist to show you the tools he or she uses. Working as a dental assistant, where you can closely observe the work of a dental hygienist, can be a valuable stepping-stone for you on your path to a dental hygienist job. This will help you to figure out how well you would do at this type of work, discuss any questions with hygienists, and enroll in a dental hygiene school, where experience as a dental assistant would certainly be helpful.

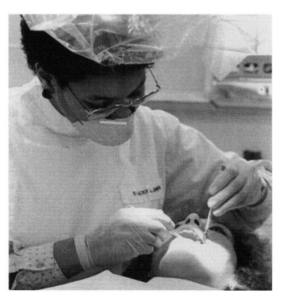
A dental hygienist cleans a patient's teeth.

American Dental Association
211 East Chicago Avenue
Chicago, IL 60611
312-440-2500
publicinfo@ada.org
http://www.ada.org

American Dental Education Association
1625 Massachusetts Avenue, NW, Suite 600
Washington, DC 20036-2212
202-667-9433
adea@adea.org
http://www.adea.org

American Dental Hygienists' Association
444 North Michigan Avenue, Suite 3400
Chicago, IL 60611
312-440-8900
mail@adha.net
http://www.adha.org

Dental Laboratory Technicians

What Dental Laboratory Technicians Do

Although patients never actually see *dental laboratory technicians,* these technicians are very important to the success of many types of dental treatments. When someone loses a tooth, for example, the dentist writes a prescription for a new one. This replacement tooth is then made by the technician in a laboratory.

There are four main kinds of laboratory work that a technician can specialize in. *Orthodontic technicians* make braces for straightening teeth by bending wires into complicated shapes that will fit over the crooked teeth. The braces, retainers, or tooth bands that these technicians make are not meant to be permanent. They will stay in a patient's mouth for a long time, however, so they must fit well and feel comfortable.

Dental ceramicists make real-looking porcelain teeth. These are made to replace missing ones or to fit over natural teeth that may have been damaged or that are just not attractive. Ceramicists apply porcelain paste over a metal frame to make crowns, bridges, and tooth coverings. Their work involves a great deal of knowledge and creativity, and they are usually the highest-paid technicians.

Some dental laboratory technicians specialize in making and repairing full and partial dentures. Full dentures are false teeth worn by people who have had all their teeth removed on the upper or lower jaw, or on both jaws. Partial dentures are the false teeth that are placed in a jaw between natural teeth to replace a missing tooth or teeth. Technicians make dentures by putting ceramic teeth in a wax model and then building up wax over it to hold the set in place.

Crown and bridge specialists restore the missing parts of a natural tooth that has been broken. They do this by using plastic and metal appliances that are permanently cemented to the natural tooth. Technicians in this area must be skilled at melting and casting metals.

SCHOOL SUBJECTS
Art, Technical/shop

MINIMUM EDUCATION LEVEL
Some postsecondary training

SALARY RANGE
$18,000 to $30,000 to $52,000

OUTLOOK
More slowly than the average

OTHER ARTICLES TO READ
Dental Assistants
Dental Hygienists
Dentists
Endodontists
Orthodontists

Most technicians work in privately owned labs that employ only about six or seven people. Many large labs specialize in one type of work, while smaller ones tend to employ technicians who perform a range of jobs.

Education and Training

In high school, classes in art (especially ceramics and sculpting) and chemistry will be helpful. All technicians must have a high school diploma.

After high school, three to four years of on-the-job training is one way to start in the profession. Another option is to complete a two-year college program in applied science. This associate's degree option is a growing trend. Courses in such a program include tooth construction, processing and repairing dentures, and making crowns.

Outlook

Although the overall demand for dental laboratory technicians is expected to grow more slowly than the average through 2012, certain job opportunities will remain favorable. Trainee positions may be readily available, but these positions do not pay well. Experienced technicians with established professional reputations can start their own laboratories to further advance their careers.

The slowing demand for dental laboratory technicians is related to the success of preventive dentistry and the widespread use of fluoridated water across the nation.

For More Information

If you are interested in a career as a dental laboratory technician, try to get a part-time

A dental laboratory technician chips off the plastic impression of a mouth to reveal the positive plaster mold.

or summer job as a laboratory helper. Talk with a dental laboratory technician, and attend seminars and lectures. Read about and practice ceramics, metal casting, and molding.

American Dental Association
Department of Career Guidance
211 East Chicago Avenue
Chicago, IL 60611
http://www.ada.org

National Association of Dental Laboratories
1530 Metropolitan Boulevard
Tallahassee, FL 32308
http://www.nadl.org

Dentists

What Dentists Do

Dentists help people to have healthy teeth and gums. They clean, fill, repair, replace, and straighten teeth. Dentists who are general practitioners do many kinds of dental work. They take X rays, fill cavities, clean teeth, and pull diseased teeth. Dentists talk to their patients about how they can prevent tooth and mouth problems and give them instructions on proper brushing, flossing, and diet.

Dentists can treat several patients a day for specific problems in addition to doing quick checks on patients who come in to see *dental hygienists* for routine cleaning. These quick checks include a physical exam of the teeth and mouth and a look at X rays. If the dentist detects a problem, he or she discusses options with the patient, who then makes one or a series of appointments.

Dentists diagnose unique problems that require the care of a dental specialist, who is devoted to just one kind of dental problem. *Orthodontists* use braces and other devices to correct irregular growth of teeth and jaws. *Oral surgeons* perform difficult tooth-pulling jobs, remove tumors, and fix broken jaws. *Periodontists* treat diseased gums. *Prosthodontists* make artificial teeth and dentures. *Pedodontists* specialize in treating children's dental problems. *Oral pathologists* examine mouth tumors and lesions and determine their causes. *Endodontists* treat patients who need root canal work.

A few dentists work for the federal government in hospitals or clinics, and others teach, conduct research, or hold positions in dental schools. However, about 90 percent of dentists have their own private practices.

Dentists who work for themselves have to handle administrative and managerial matters, such as leasing office space, hiring employees, running an office, keeping books, and stocking equipment. These dentists set their own hours, but most of them work at least 40 hours a week, including some time on weekends. For beginning dentists, it takes many hours of work to help pay for the expensive equipment they need.

SCHOOL SUBJECTS
Chemistry, Health

MINIMUM EDUCATION LEVEL
Medical degree

SALARY RANGE
$53,000 to $120,000 to $146,000

OUTLOOK
More slowly than the average

OTHER ARTICLES TO READ
Dental Assistants
Dental Hygienists
Endodontists
Orthodontists
Physicians

Education and Training

Science and math courses are a good preparation for a career in dentistry. Good vision, good manual skills, and some artistic ability are also important.

To become a dentist, you must complete three to four years of college-level predental education. Three out of four dentists have a bachelor's or master's degree.

Next, to be admitted to a certified dental school, you must pass the Dental Admissions Test. Training at a dental school then takes at least four years. During this time, you will study basic sciences, including anatomy, biochemistry, microbiology, and physiology, as well as how to treat patients.

All 50 states and the District of Columbia require dentists to be licensed. To qualify for a license in most states, a candidate must graduate from an accredited dental school pass written and practical examinations. Dentists who wish to enter a specialized field spend an additional two to three years studying that specialty.

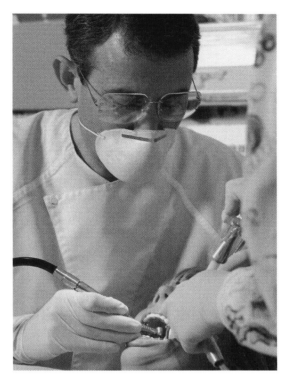

A patient complaining of tooth pain has a cavity removed by her dentist.

Outlook

Overall employment of dentists is expected to grow more slowly than the average through the next 10 years. Opportunities for specialists, such as cosmetic dentists, will be very good, especially in large metropolitan areas such as Los Angeles and Chicago.

For More Information

You can develop good manual dexterity through sculpting, metalworking, or any type of fine handwork. Volunteer in a health care facility to get experience working around patients and medical professionals.

American Dental Association
211 East Chicago Avenue
Chicago, IL 60611
312-440-2500
publicinfo@ada.org
http://www.ada.org

American Dental Education Association
1625 Massachusetts Avenue, NW, Suite 600
Washington, DC 20036-2212
202-667-9433
adea@adea.org
http://www.adea.org

Deputy U.S. Marshals

What Deputy U.S. Marshals Do

Deputy U.S. marshals are law enforcement officers who protect and enforce the decisions of the U.S. judiciary system. The judiciary system includes judges, the Supreme Court, and the Department of Justice.

Deputy U.S. marshals transport federal criminals to prison, sometimes in government-owned jets. They are on guard in federal courtrooms and protect judges and jury members who are involved in important legal cases that put their lives in possible danger. They serve subpoenas, summonses, and other legal documents.

Marshals investigate and track down fugitives (criminals who are running from the law), even those who have escaped to another country. They also try to find fugitives in the United States who are wanted by foreign nations. In hunting down fugitives, marshals often work with state and local police departments and with other law enforcement agencies.

The Marshals Service operates the nation's witness relocation program. This program encourages witnesses to testify in federal trials even though they feel that their testimony would put them in danger, such as in organized crime cases. The Marshals Service provides personal protection for the witness until he or she testifies in court. After the trial is over, the Marshals Service helps the witness move to a new city and take on a new name and identity, keeping him or her anonymous and safe from reprisals.

U.S. marshals also operate the program for confiscating property that has been purchased from the profits of certain illegal activities such as drug dealing. The marshals seize the houses, boats, and other property that criminals have purchased. They hold it and maintain it until the property is sold or put up for auction. Hundreds of millions of dollars in seized assets are in the custody of the Marshals Service.

Marshals are trained to respond to emergency situations such as riots, terrorist incidents, or hostage situations when federal law

SCHOOL SUBJECTS
Computer science, Foreign language, Government

MINIMUM EDUCATION LEVEL
High school diploma

SALARY RANGE
$32,000 to $53,000 to $84,000

OUTLOOK
Faster than the average

OTHER ARTICLES TO READ
Bounty Hunters
Customs Officials
FBI Agents
Police Officers
Secret Service Special Agents
Spies

is violated or federal property is endangered. A highly trained force of deputy U.S. marshals called the Special Operations Group is deployed in these situations.

Education and Training

Like other federal officers, deputy U.S. marshals are trained at the Federal Law Enforcement Training Center in Glynco Naval Air Station in Georgia. They complete a three-month training program that teaches them about laws, proper procedures, firearm use, and physical training.

To enter this program, you must first take a civil service exam. You are then interviewed to see if you have the makings of a good deputy marshal. You must have a minimum of some college education, work experience, or a combination of both. Any law enforcement experience and your educational level are also considered. Competition for these jobs is strong, with an average of 15 applicants for every opening.

Outlook

Changes in the Marshals Service's budget, as well as increases or decreases in the responsibilities assigned to the service, affect employment opportunities. Careers in law enforcement and security-related fields in general are expected to grow rapidly in some cases, as federal and state governments pass new tough-on-crime legislation and the number of criminals continues to grow. Threats of terrorist activity have increased security particularly in and around government offices, public buildings, airports, post offices, and media headquarters.

In spite of the continuing need for Deputy U.S. marshals, competition for avail-

During a practice drill, a deputy U.S. marshal awaits instructions from the drill leader.

able positions will remain high because of the prestige offered by this career and the generous benefits available to many careers in federal service.

For More Information

For more information about working as a deputy U.S. marshal, you can write directly to the Marshals Service. A school guidance counselor, a college or university placement office, or a public library may also have information. For more background, read Frederick S. Calhoun's book *The Lawmen: United States Marshals and Their Deputies, 1789–1989* (Smithsonian Institution Press, 1990).

U.S. Marshals Service
600 Army Navy Drive
Arlington, VA 22202-4210
202-307-9600
us.marshals@usdoj.gov
http://www.usdoj.gov/marshals

Dermatologists

SKILLS SPOTLIGHT
◆
What they do
Evaluate and manage information
Help clients and customers
Select and apply tools/technology

Skills they need
Decision making
Problem solving
Speaking/listening

What Dermatologists Do

Dermatologists study, diagnose, and treat diseases and ailments of the skin, hair, mucous membranes, nails, and related tissues or structures. They may also perform cosmetic services, such as scar removal or hair transplants.

The work of a dermatologist begins with a diagnosis to determine the cause of a disease or condition. For example, if a patient exhibits a mysterious red rash on his or her arms and legs that does not seem to go away, dermatologists determine what is wrong. They will study the patient's medical history, conduct a visual examination, and sometimes take blood samples, smears of the affected skin, microscopic scrapings, or biopsy specimens of the skin. The dermatologist may order cultures for fungi or bacteria or perform tests to find allergies or immunologic diseases. Skin, blood, or tissue samples are sent to a laboratory for testing and analysis.

Dermatologists use a variety of medicines and treatments to cure their patients. They treat some skin problems with oral medications, such as antibiotics. Certain types of inflammations of the skin, such as eczema and dermatitis, psoriasis, and acne, can be treated with creams, ointments, or other medications. Dermatologists also use ultraviolet light and radiation therapy.

Some skin problems require surgery. Dermatologists may use traditional surgery that cuts away the affected area. The skin can also be frozen (known as cryosurgery), treated with lasers, or treated with current (known as cauterization).

Many surgical procedures can be performed on an outpatient basis in the office of the dermatologist, using local anesthesia. Warts, cysts, moles, scars, and boils can all be taken care of in the office. Hair transplants and laser treatments for such problems as cysts, disfiguring birth defects, birthmarks, and spider veins can also usually be performed in a dermatologist's office.

There are many subspecialties in the field of dermatology. *Dermatoimmunologists* focus on diseases of the immune system, such as allergies. *Pediatric dermatologists* treat children with skin disorders. *Occupational dermatologists* treat occupational disorders,

---

SCHOOL SUBJECTS
Biology, Chemistry

MINIMUM EDUCATION LEVEL
Medical degree

SALARY RANGE
$43,000 to $140,000 to $146,000

OUTLOOK
About as fast as the average

OTHER ARTICLES TO READ
Cosmetic Surgeons
Cosmeticians
Electrologists
Nurses
Physicians

such as forms of dermatitis caused by biological or chemical irritants.

Education and Training

Dermatologists must first earn a bachelor's degree, take the Medical College Admission Test, and apply to a medical school. After acceptance, you must complete four years of study and training to earn a degree of Doctor of Medicine. After medical school, physicians must pass a standard examination given by the National Board of Medical Examiners. Then they begin their residency to learn their specialty. Only about half of those who apply to residency programs are accepted, and the field of dermatology is especially competitive. The American Board of Dermatology, an organization that certifies dermatologists, requires four years of residency training, three of which must be training in dermatology.

Outlook

The health care industry is thriving, and employment opportunities for physicians are expected to grow as fast as the average through 2010. The field of dermatology is expected to expand for a number of reasons. New technologies, medicines, and treatments continue to be developed at a rapid pace. Another factor in the growth of this industry is that the population is growing and aging, requiring more skin-related health care in advancing years. Demand for dermatologists has increased as people have become aware of the effects of radiation exposure from the sun and of air pollutants on skin.

Dermatologists are trained to spot skin problems.

For More Information

Tour medical settings such as hospitals, clinics, nursing homes, and health care facilities. Volunteer to work in a health care environment to get practical experience. Join science clubs that might give you an opportunity to work on biology or anatomy projects.

American Academy of Dermatology
930 North Meacham Road
Schaumburg, IL 60173-4927
http://www.aad.org

American Board of Dermatology
Henry Ford Hospital
1 Ford Place
Detroit, MI 48202-3450
http://www.abderm.org

American Medical Association
515 North State Street
Chicago, IL 60610
312-464-5000
http://www.ama-assn.org

Desktop Publishing Specialists

What Desktop Publishing Specialists Do

Have you ever made flyers to advertise a music recital? Or designed programs for a school play? Then you have probably worked with computers, desktop publishing software, scanners, and printers. *Desktop publishing specialists* do this type of work for a living. They create reports, brochures, books, magazines, newsletters, advertisements, business cards, and other documents. They work with files others have created, or they compose original text and graphics for their clients. A desktop publishing specialist is someone with artistic talent, proofreading skills, and a great deal of computer knowledge.

Desktop publishing specialists are hired by individuals, small business owners, and large companies to create a wide variety of designs for printed documents and Web pages. They use text provided by the employer and arrange it in a pleasing manner on the page or computer screen. They choose typefaces, sizes, and type styles, such as bold or italic, to emphasize certain words and phrases. They arrange column widths and check for proper spacing between letters, words, and columns.

Desktop publishing specialists create interesting graphics or use graphics or photographs supplied by the employer. They use software programs to adjust the artwork size, color, and sharpness, if necessary, and arrange it on the page to best explain, illustrate, or complement the text. They choose colors for text, artwork, and other graphic elements, such as lines, boxes, and borders.

Proofreading is an important part of this job. Desktop publishing specialists read the text of the document, checking for errors and typing errors. They examine the document for print quality and resolve any problems with resolution and color. They work closely with clients, graphic designers, printers, and copywriters to make sure they create the documents according to specifications. After the document has

SCHOOL SUBJECTS
Computer science, English

MINIMUM EDUCATION LEVEL
Some postsecondary training

SALARY RANGE
$19,000 to $31,000 to $52,000

OUTLOOK
Much faster than the average

OTHER ARTICLES TO READ
Computer Programmers
Graphic Designers
Information Brokers
Internet Content Developers
Technical Writers and Editors
Webmasters

been completed and approved, the desktop publishing specialist prepares it for posting on the Internet.

Education and Training

Desktop publishing specialists need both computer and artistic skills. Computer classes that teach graphics and page layout programs are most beneficial. Art and photography classes will teach you about color, composition, and design. English classes will help you with the editing and proofreading aspects of the job.

A college degree is not required, but many desktop publishing specialists have at least a bachelor's degree. Some community and technical colleges offer courses in desktop publishing and graphic design. A growing number of schools offer programs in technical and visual communications, which may include classes in desktop publishing, layout and design, and computer graphics. Four-year colleges also offer courses in technical communications and graphic design.

Outlook

The demand for desktop publishing specialists is expected to grow rapidly over the next several years. Electronic processes have replaced most of the manual processes performed by paste-up workers, typesetters, photoengravers, camera operators, film strippers, and platemakers.

For More Information

Become familiar with various graphic design and page layout programs. If you subscribe to an Internet service, take advantage of any free Web space available to you and design your own home page. Join

Desktop publishers work under constant deadlines.

computer clubs, and volunteer to produce newsletters and flyers for your school or church. Experience with the school paper and yearbook will help you learn about page layout, typesetting, word processing, and how to meet deadlines.

Graphic Arts Information Network
http://www.gain.org

Graphic Arts Technical Foundation
200 Deer Run Road
Sewickley, PA 15143-2600
800-910-GATF
info@gatf.org
http://www.gatf.org

Society for Technical Communication
901 North Stuart Street, Suite 904
Arlington, VA 22203-1822
703-522-4114
stc@stc.org
http://www.stc.org

Detectives

What Detectives Do

Detectives are plainclothes police officers who investigate crimes already committed and try to prevent crimes that are expected to occur. They observe people and events and collect information from various sources. The majority of detectives spend three to five years as uniformed police officers before being promoted to a detective position. Police detectives work on cases involving murder, arson, fraud, assault, and property crimes. Some specialize in one area, such as fingerprinting or handwriting analysis. Police detectives may be assigned as many as two or three cases a day, and having 30 cases to handle at one time is not unusual.

Police detectives have several ways of gathering information and evidence on crimes and suspects. For example, they contact and interview victims and witnesses, familiarize themselves with the scene of the crime and places where a suspect may spend time, and conduct surveillance operations. Detectives sometimes have informers who provide important leads. Also helpful are existing police files on other crimes, on known criminals, and on people suspected of criminal activity. If sufficient evidence has been collected, the police detective arrests the suspect, sometimes with the help of uniformed police officers.

Once a suspect is in custody, police detectives conduct an interrogation. Questioning the suspect may reveal new evidence and help determine whether the suspect was involved in other unsolved crimes. Before finishing the case, the detective prepares a detailed written report. Detectives are sometimes required to present evidence at the trial of the suspect.

Good detectives are very observant and can remember faces, names, and anything unusual about a suspected criminal, such as a peculiar way of dressing or speaking. Detectives often work in teams, but they also must be able to work independently and without constant supervision.

Narcotic squad detectives try to apprehend those who deal illegal drugs. They know how to recognize and test narcotics,

SCHOOL SUBJECTS
Government, History

MINIMUM EDUCATION LEVEL
High school diploma

SALARY RANGE
$31,000 to $51,000 to $80,000

OUTLOOK
Faster than the average

OTHER ARTICLES TO READ
Crime Analysts
Deputy U.S. Marshals
FBI Agents
Forensic Experts
Police Officers
Secret Service Special Agents
Spies

Detectives investigate a murder in New York City.

keep a trail of evidence, and seal it. They know self-defense, how to use a search warrant, and how to seize property. They sometimes have to infiltrate a suspected drug operation by pretending to be interested buyers themselves. This is called a sting operation, and it can be very dangerous, especially if the detective's true identity is revealed to the dealer.

Education and Training

To become a detective you need a high school diploma and preferably at least two years of college. Many police departments encourage candidates to attend special police academies or universities with courses in law enforcement.

You must be at least 21 years old and pass rigorous physical exams, including tests of strength and agility as well as vision. Your background will be investigated to make sure you have not committed any crimes. Once you have joined the police force, basic training is provided. After you have demonstrated solid capabilities as a police officer, you can be considered for promotion to a detective position.

Outlook

Employment for police detectives is expected to increase faster than the average in the next few years. Job openings for narcotics squad detectives are expected to continue attracting a large number of applicants.

Detectives who work as private investigators are also expected to have excellent employment opportunities. The use of private investigators by insurance firms, restaurants, hotels, and other businesses is on the rise. An area of particular growth is the investigation of the various forms of computer fraud.

For More Information

If you are interested in becoming a detective, talk with your local police department, a private investigation school, or a college or university that offers police science, criminal justice, or law enforcement courses.

International Association of Chiefs of Police
515 North Washington Street
Alexandria, VA 22314-2357
703-836-6767
information@theiacp.org
http://www.theiacp.org

National Association of Investigative Specialists
PO Box 33244
Austin, TX 78764
512-719-3595
http://www.pimall.com/nais/nais.j.html

Diagnostic Medical Sonographers

What Diagnostic Medical Sonographers Do

Diagnostic medical sonographers, or *sonographers,* use electronic instruments that record high-frequency sound waves to produce images of internal organs in the human body. These sound waves are similar to sonar, which is used to locate objects beneath the water.

Sonographers work on the orders of a physician. They set up the ultrasound equipment for each exam. They describe the imaging process to the patient as they position the patient's body correctly for the procedure. It is important to be able to put people at ease and be kind and compassionate while maintaining a professional attitude. Patients often are very old or young, or fearful about the sonogram, and they need to be reassured and comforted before the procedure begins.

When the patient is properly positioned, the sonographer applies a type of gel to the skin over the organ that will be examined. This gel improves the ability to see the image. The sonographer then moves the transducer, a device that directs sound waves, slowly over the area to be imaged and monitors the sound wave display screen to ensure that a quality ultrasonic image is being produced. The diagnostic data are recorded on computer disk, magnetic tape, strip printout, film, or videotape. When the procedure is complete, the sonographer prepares the recorded images and makes notes for the attending physician about what occurred during the exam.

Other duties of sonographers include maintaining patient records, monitoring and adjusting sonographic equipment for accuracy, and, after considerable experience, serving as supervisors, preparing work schedules, and evaluating future equipment purchases.

Education and Training

Middle and high school students should focus on the sciences, including chemistry,

SCHOOL SUBJECTS
Biology, Chemistry

MINIMUM EDUCATION LEVEL
Associate's degree

SALARY RANGE
$36,000 to $49,000 to $67,000

OUTLOOK
Faster than the average

OTHER ARTICLES TO READ
Cardiovascular Technologists
Dialysis Technicians
Electroneurodiagnostic Technicians
Medical Assistants
Respiratory Therapists
X-ray Technologists

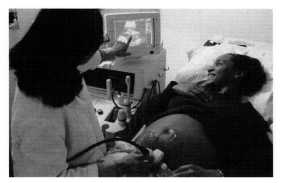
A diagnostic medical sonographer operates ultrasound equipment, in this case showing a mother-to-be an image of her fetus.

anatomy and physiology, and physics, and also mathematics, speech, and technical writing classes.

Sonographers receive their training from teaching hospitals, colleges and universities, technical schools, or the armed forces. Most sonographers enter the field after completing an associate's degree, but certificate programs and four-year bachelor's degree programs are also available.

After completing their degrees, sonographers may register with the American Registry of Diagnostic Medical Sonographers and become certified, which is optional but frequently required by employers. Other licensing requirements may exist at the state level but vary greatly.

Outlook

The use of diagnostic medical sonography, like many other imaging fields, will continue to grow because of its safe, nonradioactive imaging and its success in detecting life-threatening diseases and in analyzing previously nonimageable internal organs.

Sonography will play an increasing role in the fields of obstetrics/gynecology and cardiology. Furthermore, the aging population will create high demand for qualified technologists to operate diagnostic machinery. Demand for qualified diagnostic medical sonographers exceeds the current supply in some areas of the country, especially rural communities, small towns, and some retirement areas.

For More Information

Visit a hospital, clinic, nursing home, or other health care facility to view the equipment and facilities used and to watch professionals at work. Your guidance counselor or science teacher may be able to arrange a presentation by a sonographer.

American Registry of Diagnostic Medical Sonographers
600 Jefferson Plaza, Suite 360
Rockville, MD 20852-1150
800-541-9754
http://www.ardms.org

Commission on Accreditation of Allied Health Education Programs
35 East Wacker Drive, Suite 1970
Chicago, IL 60601-2208
312-553-9355
caahep@caahep.org
http://www.caahep.org

Society of Diagnostic Medical Sonography
2745 N Dallas Parkway, Suite 350
Plano, TX 75093-8729
800-229-9506
http://www.sdms.org

Dialysis Technicians

SKILLS SPOTLIGHT
◆
What they do
Evaluate and manage information
Help clients and customers
Work with a team

Skills they need
Problem solving
Responsibility
Self-management

What Dialysis Technicians Do

Dialysis technicians, also called *nephrology technicians* or *renal dialysis technicians,* set up and operate hemodialysis (artificial kidney) machines for patients whose kidneys have failed. Dialysis technicians also maintain and repair equipment as well as educate patients and their families about dialysis. All dialysis technicians work under the supervision of physicians or registered nurses.

Healthy kidneys remove toxic wastes from our blood in the form of urine. Chronic renal failure is a condition in which the kidneys cease to perform this task. Many people, especially diabetics or people who suffer from undetected high blood pressure, develop this condition. These patients require hemodialysis to stay alive. In hemodialysis the patient's blood is circulated through the dialysis machine, which takes over for the kidneys by filtering out impurities, wastes, and excess fluids from the blood. The cleaned blood is then returned to the patient's body.

Dialysis technicians most often work in a hospital or special dialysis center. Some technicians travel to patients' homes. Technicians prepare the patient for dialysis, monitor the procedure, and respond to any emergencies that occur during the treatment. Before dialysis, the technician measures the patient's vital signs (including weight, pulse, blood pressure, and temperature) and obtains blood samples and specimens as required. The technician then inserts tubes into a vein or a catheter, through which blood is exchanged between the patient and the artificial kidney machine.

The dialysis process usually takes about three hours. During this time, technicians keep a close watch on the patients and the machines. They must be attentive, precise, and alert. They measure and adjust blood-flow rates as well as check and recheck the patient's vital signs. All of this information is carefully recorded in a log. In addition, technicians must respond to any alarms that occur during the procedure

SCHOOL SUBJECTS
Biology, Chemistry

MINIMUM EDUCATION LEVEL
Some postsecondary training

SALARY RANGE
$21,000 to $34,000 to $57,000

OUTLOOK
Faster than the average

OTHER ARTICLES TO READ
Cardiovascular Technologists
Diagnostic Medical Sonographers
Medical Assistants
Respiratory Therapists
X-ray Technologists

and make appropriate adjustments on the dialysis machine.

Education and Training

To become a dialysis technician, you need at least a high school diploma or the equivalent. Previous experience caring for the seriously ill, such as volunteering in a hospital, is highly recommended. There are only a few two-year dialysis preparatory programs available in technical schools and junior colleges. Most technicians learn their skills through on-the-job training.

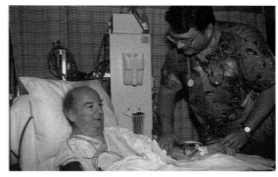

Dialysis technicians must be skilled at operating their equipment, but they also must be able to put patients at ease and make them comfortable.

Outlook

There should continue to be a need for dialysis technicians in the future as the number of people with kidney disease and failure increases. Those with kidney failure must have either dialysis or a kidney transplant in order to live. The steadily increasing number of patients in need will mean a continued strong demand for dialysis technicians.

Technicians make up the largest proportion of the dialysis team, since they can care for only a limited number of patients at a time. There is also a high turnover rate in the field of dialysis technicians, creating many new job openings, and there is a shortage of trained dialysis technicians in most localities.

For More Information

Volunteering in a hospital, nursing home, dialysis center, or other patient-care facility can give you experience in caring for patients. Most hospitals have volunteer programs that are open to high school students. If you have a family member, neighbor, or friend who is on dialysis, ask if you can come along to observe. Most dialysis patients appreciate having visitors.

American Nephrology Nurses' Association
East Holly Avenue, Box 56
Pitman, NJ 08071-0056
888-600-2662
anna@ajj.com
http://anna.inurse.com

National Association of Nephrology Technicians/Technologists
PO Box 2307
Dayton, OH 45401-2307
937-586-3705
nant@nant.meinet.com
http://www.dialysistech.org

National Kidney Foundation
30 East 33rd Street, Suite 1100
New York, NY 10016
800-622-9010
http://www.kidney.org

Diesel Mechanics

What Diesel Mechanics Do

Diesel mechanics work on the diesel engines that power buses, ships, automobiles, trucks, locomotives, construction machinery, and farm and highway equipment. Their work can be divided into three basic categories: maintenance, repair, and rebuilding.

Maintenance work involves the day-to-day servicing that keeps the engine running smoothly. This includes checking oil levels, the brake system, steering mechanisms, and wheel bearings; cleaning air and oil filters; removing and checking the various parts of the fuel system; and inspecting the water cooling system.

Despite regular maintenance checks, parts of the engine can wear out or break. When this happens, the mechanic removes, replaces, and adjusts the defective part.

To rebuild an engine a diesel mechanic must take it completely apart. This is usually scheduled at regular intervals, such as every 18 months or 100,000 miles.

Mechanics use a variety of instruments to check each part and then either repair, adjust, or replace it as needed. Diesel mechanics use specialty instruments to make precision measurements and diagnostics of each engine component. Micrometers and various gauges test for engine wear. Ohmmeters, ammeters, and voltmeters test electrical components. Dynamometers and oscilloscopes test overall engine operations.

The work of diesel mechanics varies according to the kind of machine they are working on. Most diesel mechanics work on the engines of heavy trucks, such as those used in hauling freight over long distances. All mechanics know the principles of diesel engines and are prepared to do exacting, often strenuous work to keep engines in good working order. They usually work indoors and are exposed to dirt and grease. Diesel mechanics work with heavy tools such as welding and flame-cutting equipment, power wrenches, lathes, and grinding machines. Shops must comply with strict safety procedures to help employees avoid accidents.

SCHOOL SUBJECTS
Computer science, Technical/shop

MINIMUM EDUCATION LEVEL
High school diploma

SALARY RANGE
$23,000 to $35,000 to $52,000

OUTLOOK
About as fast as the average

OTHER ARTICLES TO READ
Automobile Collision Repairers
Automobile Detailers
Automobile Mechanics
Automobile Sales Workers
Automotive Industry Workers

Education and Training

Entry-level diesel mechanics need a high school diploma, a Class A driver's license, and they must complete some formal training. Training can vary from on-the-job or apprenticeship training to formal classroom work in a technical or vocational school that offers courses in diesel equipment. Because of the time and money it takes to train an apprentice, most employers today prefer to hire only those who have some postsecondary training.

Many diesel mechanics begin their training by working on gasoline engines. Many gain experience working on cars as a weekend or part-time job when they are in high school. Some firms, particularly those that manufacture diesel engines, offer their own formal training programs, which can last from six months to four years.

Outlook

Employment for diesel mechanics is expected to grow about as fast as the average in the next 10 years. Most jobs for diesel

Three mechanics assemble a marine diesel engine.

mechanics will be with trucking companies that hire mechanics to maintain and repair their fleets. Construction companies are also expected to require an increase in diesel mechanics to maintain their heavy machinery, such as cranes, earthmovers, and other diesel-powered equipment.

For More Information

Many community centers offer general auto maintenance workshops where you can get practice working on cars and learn from instructors.

Trade magazines such as *Landline* (http://www.landlinemag.com) and *Overdrive* (http://www.overdriveonline.com) are an excellent source for learning what's new in the trucking industry and can be found at libraries and some larger bookstores.

Automotive Aftermarket Industry Association
4600 East-West Highway, Suite 300
Bethesda, MD 20814-3415
301-654-6664
aaia@aftermarket.org
http://www.aftermarket.org

Inter-Industry Conference on Auto Collision Repair
3701 Algonquin Road, Suite 400
Rolling Meadows, IL 60008
800-422-7872
http://www.i-car.com

National Institute for Automotive Service Excellence
101 Blue Seal Drive, Suite 101
Leesburg, VA 20175
703-669-6650
877-ASE-TECH
http://www.asecert.org

Diet and Fitness Writers

What Diet and Fitness Writers Do

Diet and fitness writers express, edit, promote, and interpret ideas and facts about nutrition and exercise in written form for books, magazines, Web sites, trade journals, newspapers, technical studies and reports, and company newsletters. The word "diet" actually refers to the food one eats regularly, not a restrictive eating plan. Diet and fitness writers analyze healthy diets, frequently high in protein and low in saturated fats, and evaluate poor diets, often characterized as high in sugar and saturated fats.

These writers may report on their own experiences, or they may write about the diet or sports activities of others. Some diet and fitness writers create articles or full books on new dieting methods or exercise forms to persuade the public to adopt that dieting or fitness trend.

They may write health and fitness articles for books, magazines, and journals.

They also contribute to scientific research and technical reports. Many writers promote popular diets or fitness fads. They may write advertisement copy or contribute to health and fitness segments for radio and television broadcasts.

Diet and fitness writers can be employed either as in-house staff or as freelancers. Pay varies according to experience and position, but freelancers must provide their own office space, health insurance, and equipment such as computers and fax machines.

Many diet and fitness writers also work as personal trainers, dietitians, or nutritionists, or in other related careers.

Education and Training

While in high school, build a broad educational foundation by taking courses in English, literature, health, science, computer science, and typing.

Competition for writing jobs in the diet and fitness arena is very strong. A college

---

SCHOOL SUBJECTS
English, Health, Physical education

MINIMUM EDUCATION LEVEL
Bachelor's degree

SALARY RANGE
$23,000 to $44,000 to $91,000

OUTLOOK
About as fast as the average

OTHER ARTICLES TO READ
Copy Editors
Copywriters
Dietetic Technicians
Dietitians and Nutritionists
Sportswriters
Writers

---

education may not be required, but it helps to establish your skills as a writer. If you want to be hired full-time as a diet or fitness writer, employers may prefer that you have a background in nutrition or sports fitness as well as course work in English or journalism. Some highly technical journals or scientific research publications require their writers to have a master's degree.

In addition to formal course work, most employers look for practical writing experience. Experience with high school and college newspapers, yearbooks, and literary magazines will make you a better candidate. In addition, experience or internships with a small community newspaper, radio station, or local television station is also valuable.

Outlook

The employment of all writers is expected to increase at a rate about as fast as the average for all occupations through 2012, according to the U.S. Department of Labor. The demand for writers by newspapers, periodicals, book publishers, and nonprofit organizations is expected to increase. The growth of online publishing will also demand many talented writers; those with computer skills will have an advantage as a result.

People entering this field should realize that the competition for jobs is extremely keen, especially for writers beginning their careers. Ultimately, many aspiring writers, including diet and fitness writers, turn to other occupations when they find that applicants far outnumber the job openings available.

Bellydancing is one of the newest trends to hit the exercise circuit. This diet and fitness writer samples a class before writing on this growing trend.

For More Information

As an elementary or middle school student, you can test your interest and skills in the writing field by serving as a reporter or writer on school newspapers, yearbooks, and literary magazines. You should also explore the field of fitness and nutrition by participating in sports and taking part in health clinics or workshops.

American Council on Exercise
4851 Paramount Drive
San Diego, CA 92123
800-825-3636
http://www.acefitness.org

American Dietetic Association
120 South Riverside Plaza, Suite 2000
Chicago, IL 60606-6995
800-877-1600
http://www.eatright.org

Association for Education in Journalism and Mass Communication
234 Outlet Pointe Boulevard
Columbia SC 29210-5667
803-798-0271
http://www.aejmc.org

Dietetic Technicians

What Dietetic Technicians Do

Dietetic technicians work in two areas: food-service management and nutritional care of individuals (also called clinical nutrition). They usually work as members of a team under the direction of a dietitian. Most technicians work for hospitals and nursing homes. Others work for health agencies such as public health departments or neighborhood health centers.

Technicians who work in food-service management perform a variety of tasks. They work in the kitchen overseeing the actual food preparation, or they supervise dietetic aides who serve food to patients in the cafeteria and in their hospital rooms. Technicians also manage the work and time schedules of other food-service employees. In addition, they train employees and evaluate their work. Technicians sometimes develop recipes as well as diet plans for patients. They also help patients select their menus. Some have the duties of keeping track of food items on hand, ordering supplies, and supervising food storage.

Technicians must be able to give full attention to the details of their own job while coordinating the work of other employees.

Technicians involved in clinical nutrition work under the supervision of a dietitian. They interview patients about their eating habits and the foods they prefer. This information is given to the dietitian along with reports on each patient's progress. Patients' histories reveal any need for changes in their diets, in which case the technician also teaches patients and their families about good nutrition. Technicians also keep in touch with patients after they leave the hospital to see if they are staying on their diets.

Some dietetic technicians work in community programs. They teach families how to buy and prepare healthful foods, or they work with patients who have special diet needs, such as the elderly. Some technicians work in programs that provide meals for the needy.

Dietetic technicians also work for schools, colleges, and industrial food-service companies. Some work in research

---

SCHOOL SUBJECTS
Biology, Chemistry

MINIMUM EDUCATION LEVEL
Associate's degree

SALARY RANGE
$15,000 to $23,000 to $36,000

OUTLOOK
About as fast as the average

OTHER ARTICLES TO READ
Cooks, Chefs, and Bakers
Dietitians and Nutritionists
Family and Consumer Scientists
Food Production Workers
Food Technologists

kitchens under the supervision of a dietitian. These technicians keep track of supplies, weigh and package food items, inspect equipment, and keep records.

Education and Training

Dietetic technicians must have a high school diploma and complete a two-year program approved by the American Dietetic Association that leads to an associate's degree. Such programs combine classroom work with on-the-job experience. Subjects studied include food science, menu planning, sanitation and safety, and diseases related to poor nutrition. You also learn how to purchase, store, prepare, and serve food.

Voluntary certification is offered by the American Dietetic Association. You must complete an approved education program and take an examination to earn the Dietetic Technician, Registered designation.

Outlook

Employment for dietetic technicians is expected to grow about as fast as the average through 2012. Most Americans place great importance on nutrition and health, and more nutritional health services will be used in future years. The population is growing, and the percentage of older people, who need the most health services, is increasing even faster.

Another reason for the positive outlook for technicians is that health care organizations now realize the advantages of hiring them for a variety of jobs. Many of the tasks dietitians used to perform can be done well by dietetic technicians, at lower cost to employers, leaving dietitians to do specialized work.

A dietetic technician offers a patient tips on good nutrition.

For More Information

Volunteer and part-time jobs may be available in the food-service department of a hospital or other health care organization near you. Also consider volunteering for community programs, such as food pantries or food service for the homeless, or for organizations that prepare and deliver meals to the elderly and homebound.

American Dietetic Association
216 West Jackson Boulevard, Suite 800
Chicago, IL 60606-6995
education@eatright.org
http://www.eatright.org

American Society for Nutritional Sciences
9650 Rockville Pike, Suite 4500
Bethesda, MD 20814
http://www.asns.org

Center for Nutrition Policy and Promotion
http://www.usda.gov/cnpp

International and American Associations of Clinical Nutritionists
16775 Addison Road, Suite 100
Addison, TX 75001
http://www.iaacn.org

Dietitians and Nutritionists

What Dietitians and Nutritionists Do

Dietitians and *nutritionists* advise people on eating habits and plan diets that will improve or maintain their health. They work for themselves or for institutions such as hospitals, schools, restaurants, and hotels. *Registered dietitians* (RDs) have completed strict training and testing requirements designed by the American Dietetic Association. Nutritionists include people with various levels of training and skills. Regulations covering the use of this title vary from state to state. *Certified clinical nutritionists* (CCNs) have the same core educational and internship backgrounds as RDs. Yet, they are specialists who have completed some postgraduate education that focuses on the biochemical and physiological aspects of nutrition science.

Clinical dietitians plan and supervise the preparation of diets designed for patients, and they work for hospitals and retirement homes. In many cases, patients cannot eat certain foods for medical reasons, such as diabetes or liver failure, and dietitians see that these patients receive nourishing meals. They work closely with doctors, who advise them regarding their patients' health and the foods that the patients cannot eat.

Community dietitians usually work for clinics, government health programs, social service agencies, or similar organizations. They counsel individuals or advise the members of certain groups about nutritional problems, proper eating, and sensible grocery shopping.

Although most nutritionists do some kind of teaching in the course of their work, teaching nutritionists specialize in education. They usually work for hospitals, and they may teach full time or part time. Sometimes, teaching nutritionists also perform other tasks, such as running a food-service operation, especially in small colleges.

CCNs typically work in private practice for themselves, as part of a group of health care professionals, or for a doctor or doctors in private practice. They work with

SCHOOL SUBJECTS
Family and consumer science, Health

MINIMUM EDUCATION LEVEL
Bachelor's degree

SALARY RANGE
$26,000 to $41,000 to $59,000

OUTLOOK
About as fast as the average

OTHER ARTICLES TO READ
Cooks, Chefs, and Bakers
Dietetic Technicians
Food Production Workers
Food Technologists
Herbalists
Naturopaths

During a meeting with a client, a nutritionist discusses healthy meal options.

clients to correct imbalances in the clients' biochemistry and improve their physiological function.

Education and Training

There are no specific educational requirements for nutritionists who are not dietitians, but most nutritionists have at least two years of college-level training in nutrition, food service, or another related subject.

To become a registered dietitian, you must have a bachelor's degree, complete a practice program that takes six to 12 months, and pass an examination. After that, you must complete continuing-education courses so that you can stay registered.

To be eligible for many positions in institutions, you must be an RD, a CCN, or a registered dietetic technician. If you want to teach, do research, or work in the field of public health, you will need one or more advanced degrees.

Outlook

Employment of dietitians and nutritionists is expected to grow about as fast as the average over the next 10 years. The public is increasingly aware of the importance of nutrition, and people are consulting with experts for nutritional advice. Dietitians working in hospitals, nursing care facilities, and state government may experience slower growth than others in the industry. Many hospitals, nursing care facilities, and state governments are expected to hire contractors to handle food-service operations.

For More Information

Learn healthy ways to cook and bake. Plan and prepare meals for your family. Do your own grocery shopping, and learn to pick out the best produce, meats, fish, and other ingredients. Take cooking classes offered by your school and other organizations in your community.

American Dietetic Association
216 West Jackson Boulevard, Suite 800
Chicago, IL 60606-6995
312-899-0040
http://www.eatright.org

American Society for Nutritional Sciences
9650 Rockville Pike, Suite 4500
Bethesda, MD 20814
301-530-7050
http://www.asns.org

Disc Jockeys

What Disc Jockeys Do

Disc jockeys, or *DJs*, play recorded music on the radio or during parties, dances, and special occasions. On the radio, they also announce the time, the weather forecast, and important news. Sometimes DJs interview guests and make public service announcements.

Unlike radio and television newscasters, disc jockeys most often do not have to read from a written script. Their comments are usually spontaneous, except when they read scripted commercials. They play musical selections, fading them out when necessary to make room for commercials, news, time and traffic checks, or weather reports.

Because most radio shows are live broadcasts and anything may happen while they are on the air, disc jockeys must react calmly under stress and know how to handle unexpected circumstances. The best disc jockeys have pleasant, soothing voices and a talent for keeping listeners entertained.

Often, disc jockeys have irregular hours, and most of them work alone. Some have to report for work at a very early hour in the morning or work late into the night because so many radio stations broadcast 24 hours per day. Despite their challenging schedules, disc jockeys' work can be exciting. Some DJs who stay with a station for a long time become famous local personalities. After they have become well known, they might be invited to participate in civic activities and charity events.

Because disc jockeys play the music their listeners like and talk about the things their listeners want to talk about, they are always aware of pleasing their audience. If listeners switch stations, ratings go down, and disc jockeys can lose their jobs.

Some disc jockeys work at parties and other special events on a part-time basis.

Education and Training

There is no formal education required of a disc jockey. However, many large stations prefer to hire people who have had some college education. Some schools train students for broadcasting, but such training

---

SCHOOL SUBJECTS
English, Speech

MINIMUM EDUCATION LEVEL
Some postsecondary training

SALARY RANGE
$13,000 to $22,000 to $54,000

OUTLOOK
Decline

OTHER ARTICLES TO READ
Actors
Broadcast Engineers
Radio and Television Announcers
Radio and Television Program Directors
Radio Producers

will not necessarily improve one's chances of finding a job at a radio station.

If you are interested in becoming a disc jockey and advancing to other broadcasting positions, you should attend a school that will train you to become an announcer. Alternatively, you can apply for any job at a radio station and try to work your way up until you are given an on-air position.

Outlook

Employment of announcers is expected to decline slightly in the future, so competition for jobs will be great in an already competitive field.

While small stations will still hire beginners, on-air experience will be increasingly important. Another area where job seekers can push ahead of the competition is in specialization. Knowledge of specific areas such as business, consumer, and health news may be advantageous.

Radio station mergers and changes in the industry can affect employment. If a radio station has to make cuts due to the economy, it is most likely to do so in a behind-the-scenes area, which means that the disc jockeys may have to take on additional duties.

For More Information

Take advantage of any opportunity you get to speak or perform before an audience. Volunteer or audition for emcee duties at special events at your school, church, or community center. Join a debate team or forensics club to work on your speaking skills. Volunteer for organizations that make recordings for the visually impaired. You will provide a valuable service while being able to practice cold-reading on tape.

A disc jockey announces the next recording to be played on his radio show.

Broadcast Education Association
1771 N Street, NW
Washington, DC 20036-2891
202-429-5354
http://www.beaweb.org

National Association of Broadcasters
1771 N Street, NW
Washington, DC 20036
202-429-5300
http://www.nab.org

National Association of Broadcast Employees and Technicians
501 Third Street, NW, 8th Floor
Washington, DC 20001
202-434-1254
http://nabetcwa.org

Radio–Television News Directors Association and Foundation
1600 K Street, NW, Suite 700
Washington, DC 20006-2838
202-659-6510
http://www.rtnda.org

Dispensing Opticians

What Dispensing Opticians Do

Dispensing opticians measure and fit clients with prescription eyeglasses, contact lenses, other low-vision aids, and sometimes artificial eyes. They help clients select appropriate frames and order all necessary ophthalmic laboratory work.

Dispensing opticians may work in the optical department of a large department store or in a small store that sells only eyewear. Some dispensing opticians work for ophthalmologists or optometrists who sell glasses to their patients.

Dispensing opticians help customers select frames for their glasses. They consider the customer's work and activities, facial characteristics, comfort, and the thickness of the corrective lenses. After the frames are chosen, the optician measures the distance between the customer's pupils and determines exactly where the lenses should be placed in relation to the pupils of the eyes.

The dispensing optician then prepares work orders for the ophthalmic laboratory. Opticians record lens prescriptions, lens size, and the style and color of the frames. They send the orders to the laboratory, where technicians grind the lenses and insert them into the frames. Sometimes the laboratory is located right on the premises, and sometimes the prescription must be sent to an outside laboratory.

When the glasses are ready, dispensing opticians make sure the prescription is correct and that the glasses fit the customer properly. They use small hand tools to adjust the frames so the lenses are positioned correctly and the frames are comfortable.

Some dispensing opticians fit contact lenses as well as glasses. They measure the curve of the customer's eye and then give these measurements and the doctor's prescription to an optics technician, who makes the lenses. Dispensing opticians also teach customers how to wear and care for the lenses.

SCHOOL SUBJECTS
Biology, Business, Mathematics

MINIMUM EDUCATION LEVEL
Apprenticeship

SALARY RANGE
$16,000 to $26,000 to $43,000

OUTLOOK
About as fast as the average

OTHER ARTICLES TO READ
Ophthalmic Laboratory Technicians
Ophthalmologists
Optical Engineers
Optometric Technicians
Optometrists
Retail Business Owners

A dispensing optician assists a patient trying on glasses.

Education and Training

To become a dispensing optician, you must first earn a high school diploma. Mathematics, health, and mechanical drawing classes are helpful.

Many dispensing opticians learn on the job as apprentices, and some companies that sell glasses offer apprenticeship programs that last two to four years. However, more employers prefer to hire those who have graduated from two-year college programs. Community colleges and trade schools offer two-year optician programs that teach the science of optics and the techniques of making lenses as well as business and communications. Dispensing opticians need special training to fit contact lenses. This training is usually offered by contact lens manufacturers.

In some states, dispensing opticians must have a license to fit glasses. To earn the license, you must usually pass an oral and a written exam. Dispensing opticians must have good hand-eye coordination and the ability to work well with customers.

Outlook

The demand for dispensing opticians will grow as fast as the average in the next 10 years. One reason for this steady growth is an increase in the number of people who need corrective eyeglasses. More than 60 percent of the people in the United States now wear prescription glasses or contact lenses. Dispensing opticians and others involved with eye care continue to develop ways of making corrective lenses more comfortable, attractive, and easy to wear.

For More Information

Visit optical shops in your area. During slow periods, opticians may be willing to talk to you about their jobs. Ask if you can tour a laboratory to see how glasses are made.

American Board of Opticianry/National Contact Lens Examiners
6506 Loisdale Road, Suite 209
Springfield, VA 22150
703-719-5800
http://www.abo.org

Commission on Opticianry Accreditation
8665 Sudley Road, #341
Manassas, Virginia 20110
703-940-9134
info@coaccreditation.com
http://www.coaccreditation.com

National Academy of Opticianry
8401 Corporate Drive, Suite 605
Landover, MD 20785
800-229-4828
http://www.nao.org

Opticians Association of America
441 Carlisle Drive
Herndon Virginia 20170
703-437-8780
oaa@oaa.org
http://www.oaa.org

Divers and Diving Technicians

What Divers and Diving Technicians Do

Divers and *diving technicians* are experts who use scuba gear (an oxygen tank and breathing apparatus) to perform underwater work. They inspect, repair, remove, and install underwater equipment and structures. They work on underwater research projects, building and maintaining oil wells and other submerged structures.

Most divers work for commercial diving contractors who take on a wide variety of jobs, including building underwater foundations for bridges, placing offshore oil well piping, and fixing damaged ships, barges, or permanent structures located in the water.

Divers and diving technicians must not only be skilled at diving but also must be able to do a variety of tasks both underwater and aboard a sailing vessel. They may have to repair a hole in a ship while it is in the water or search for missing equipment at sea. Many divers and diving technicians work on research projects investigating life in the lakes and oceans. They may take underwater photographs or make films or videotapes. Some work on salvage projects, such as exploring and retrieving items from wrecked ships at sea. Others help with underwater military projects.

Divers must be able to use hand tools, such as hammers, wrenches, and metal-cutting equipment while deep underwater, and they must use air compressors and breathing-gas storage tanks. They carry communications equipment that allows them to receive instructions from workers on the boat and to receive alerts to any developing problems.

They often work in teams and must always be aware of what is going on around them and how much oxygen remains in their tanks. Some divers and diving technicians are recreation specialists who teach scuba diving lessons or coordinate diving programs for resorts or cruise ships.

SCHOOL SUBJECTS
Physical education, Technical/shop

MINIMUM EDUCATION LEVEL
High school diploma

SALARY RANGE
$23,000 to $34,000 to $59,000

OUTLOOK
About as fast as the average

OTHER ARTICLES TO READ
Construction Laborers
Marine Biologists
Merchant Mariners
Oceanographers
Petroleum Engineers and Technicians
Petroleum Refining Workers
Photographers

Education and Training

The best way to prepare for a diving career is to complete a two-year training program. To enter a diving program, you must have a high school diploma, with mathematics and science skills, and good health. You must be an excellent swimmer and have the coordination to perform complicated tasks underwater.

The two-year program has classes in diving techniques and the skills needed to work underwater. Programs for recreation specialists also include training in business and communication.

Certification is required for recreation specialists. Certification for commercial divers is not required but is available through the Association of Commercial Divers International.

Outlook

The world is increasingly turning to the sea to supply mineral resources, new and additional sources of food and medicine, transportation, and national defense. This growth in marine activity has resulted in a continuing demand for qualified divers and diving technicians. Entry-level positions can be low-paying and mostly on dry land. Nevertheless, with a few years of experience, gradually spending more time in the water and learning skills on the job, divers usually are rewarded in terms of both pay and job satisfaction.

For More Information

Join the swim team, or take swimming lessons. Hobbies such as boating, fishing, and water skiing allow you to spend time in and on the water. You can begin diving train-

This diver is surrounded by Sergeant Major fish in the Red Sea, Egypt.

ing before high school. Between the ages of 12 and 15 you can earn a Junior Open Water Diver certification, which allows you to dive in the company of a certified adult. When you turn 15, you can upgrade your certification to Open Water Diver.

Association of Commercial Diving Educators
c/o Marine Technology Program/
Santa Barbara City College
721 Cliff Drive
Santa Barbara, CA 93109
805-965-0581
http://www.acde.us

National Association of Underwater Instructors
PO Box 89789
Tampa, FL 33689-0413
800-553-6284
http://naui.org

# Drafters

SKILLS SPOTLIGHT
◆

What they do
Evaluate and manage information
Select and apply tools/technology
Work with a team

Skills they need
Problem solving
Reading/writing
Reasoning

What Drafters Do

Drafters are technical artists who prepare clear, complete, and accurate drawings and plans for engineering, construction, and manufacturing purposes. The drawings are based on rough sketches and calculations of engineers, architects, and industrial designers. The accuracy of drawings and plans depends on the drafter's knowledge of machinery, engineering practices, mathematics, building materials, and the physical sciences.

For example, an architect might prepare a rough sketch of an office building. The sketch shows what the building will look like and includes the measurements of its size. Before the building can be constructed, extremely detailed drawings of every part of the building must be made. These drawings, called blueprints or layouts, are created by drafters.

Senior drafters, sometimes called *chief drafters,* use the ideas of architects and engineers to make design layouts. *Detailers* make complete drawings from these design layouts. Complete drawings usually include the dimensions of the object

or structure and the type of material to be used in constructing it. *Checkers* carefully examine drawings to look for mistakes. *Tracers* correct any mistakes found by the checkers and then trace the finished drawings onto transparent cloth, paper, or plastic film. This makes the drawings easy to reproduce.

Drafters often specialize in a certain type of drawing or in a certain field. *Commercial drafters* do all-around drafting, such as plans for building sites or layouts of offices or factories. *Cartographic drafters* help with accurate mapmaking, focusing on political boundaries and borders. *Geological drafters* make diagrams and maps of geological formations and locations of mineral, oil, and gas deposits.

For many years, drafters traditionally worked at large, tilted drawing tables, with a variety of drawing instruments, including protractors, compasses, triangles, squares, drawing pens, and pencils. Today, drafters more often use sophisticated design software for computer-aided design (also

SCHOOL SUBJECTS
Art, Mathematics

MINIMUM EDUCATION LEVEL
Some postsecondary training

SALARY RANGE
$25,000 to $37,000 to $56,000

OUTLOOK
More slowly than the average

OTHER ARTICLES TO READ
Architects
Cartographers
Computer-Aided Design Technicians
Electrical and Electronics Technicians
Mechanical Engineering Technicians

called computer-aided design and drafting, or CAD).

Drafters must have good hand-eye coordination for the fine detail work involved in drafting. They also must have a good sense of spatial perception (the ability to visualize objects in two or three dimensions) and formal perception (the ability to compare and discriminate between shapes, lines, forms, and shadings).

Education and Training

Mathematics and science courses are important preparation for drafting careers. Mechanical drawing classes and wood, metal, or electric shop are also helpful.

Most beginning drafters must take classes after high school to get a job. Two-year drafting programs are offered by community colleges and vocational schools. These programs include courses in science, mathematics, drawing, sketching, and drafting techniques. More employers now look for graduates of four-year programs at technical institutes. Certification of your skills, offered by the American Design Drafting Association, the trade association for drafters, is also helpful.

Outlook

Employment for drafters is expected to grow more slowly than the average through 2012. Increasing use of CAD technology will limit the demand for less-skilled drafters, but industrial growth and more complex designs of new products and manufacturing processes will increase the demand for drafting services. Opportunities will be best for well-educated drafters.

For More Information

Take up hobbies and leisure time activities that require the preparation of drawings or use of blueprints, such as woodworking, building models, and repairing and remodeling projects. When your family purchases an item that you put together yourself, study the assembly instructions and drawings.

American Design Drafting Association
105 East Main Street
Newbern, TN 38059
731-627-0802
corporate@adda.org
http://www.adda.org

International Federation of Professional and Technical Engineers
8630 Fenton Street, Suite 400
Silver Spring, MD 20910
301-565-9016
http://www.ifpte.org

A drafter carefully fine-tunes plans for a new apartment building.

Dry Cleaning and Laundry Workers

What Dry Cleaning and Laundry Workers Do

Dry cleaning and laundry workers dry clean, wash, dry, and press clothing, linens, curtains, rugs, and other articles made from natural and synthetic fibers. This work is done for individuals, families, industries, hospitals, schools, and other institutions. In smaller laundries and dry cleaning plants, one worker may perform several different tasks. In larger plants, a worker usually performs only one job in the cleaning process.

Some laundry may be picked up from homes and businesses by *sales route drivers*. These drivers also return the laundry after it has been cleaned. Some people bring their laundry to dry cleaning stores. Here, *sales clerks* take the items from customers, add up the cleaning costs, and fill out claim tickets or receipts for the customers to bring back when they pick up their items. Clerks also inspect the articles for rips and stains, mark the items to identify the customer to whom they belong, and bundle them for cleaning.

In the cleaning plant, *markers* put tags on articles so they are not lost. Then they send the items to rooms where they are either dry cleaned or laundered. If the articles are to be dry cleaned, *classifiers* sort them according to the treatment they need. If the items are to be laundered, *sorters* weigh the items and put individual customer's articles into net bags to keep them together.

Laundry spotters brush stains with chemicals or other cleaners until the stains disappear. Plants that clean rugs may employ *rug measurers* to record the size of the rugs so they can be stretched back to their original size after cleaning.

When articles are to be cleaned, *laundry laborers* and *loaders* take the laundry to the washing machines. *Washing machine operators* then wash the articles. When the washing cycle is complete, operators load the laundry into extractors, which remove about 50 percent of the water from washed laundry. The damp laundry is then put on

---

SCHOOL SUBJECTS
Chemistry, Technical/shop

MINIMUM EDUCATION LEVEL
High school diploma

SALARY RANGE
$13,000 to $17,000 to $25,000

OUTLOOK
About as fast as the average

OTHER ARTICLES TO READ
Hotel Executive Housekeepers
Household Workers
Janitors and Cleaners
Textile Workers

a conveyor belt that takes it to dryers, conditioners, and other machines.

Dry cleaners operate the machines that use chemicals to clean items. *Hand dry cleaners* clean delicate items that need individual attention by hand.

When items are dry or semi-dry, *pressers* or *finishers* operate machines that use heat or steam to press the items. *Flatwork finishers* feed linens into automatic pressing machines. *Puff ironers* press portions of garments that cannot be ironed with a flat press by pulling them over heated, metal forms.

A dry cleaning and laundry worker performs alterations at a dry cleaning facility.

Education and Training

Most dry cleaning and laundry workers learn their skills on the job. Usually, the only educational requirement is a high school diploma or its equivalent. However, courses in sewing, textiles, and clothing construction are useful. In addition, chemistry, shop, and computer classes can be beneficial. Some large dry cleaning and laundry plants offer formal training programs for new employees.

Another way to learn dry cleaning and laundry skills is through training and seminars provided by trade associations.

Outlook

The general declining employment trends in the textile and apparel industries will not necessarily affect the large number of dry cleaning establishments in the country or the need for laundry workers in hotels, hospitals, and nursing homes. In the next 10 years, automation advances will cut the number of unskilled and semiskilled workers needed, and most openings will be for skilled workers, drivers, and managers. In the dry cleaning industry, there are many opportunities for workers who can perform pressing and spotting procedures.

For More Information

To find out more about laundry and dry cleaning work, visit a plant or institution and talk with owners and workers. Libraries are also a good source of information about this industry.

Cleaners Online
http://www.cleanersonline.com

International Fabricare Institute
14700 Sweitzer Lane
Laurel, MD 20707
800-638-2627
techline@ifi.org
http://www.ifi.org

Neighborhood Cleaners Association International
252 West 29th Street
New York, NY 10001
800-888-1622
http://www.nca-i.com

Drywall Installers and Finishers

What Drywall Installers and Finishers Do

Drywall panels consist of a thin layer of plaster between two sheets of heavy paper. The panels are used in place of wet plaster to make the inside walls and ceilings of houses and other buildings. *Drywall installers* measure the areas to be covered and then mark the panels and cut them. They use a keyhole saw to cut openings for electrical outlets, vents, and plumbing fixtures. Next, they fit the pieces of drywall into place and use glue to attach them to the wooden framework. Then they nail or screw them down. Installers usually need a helper to assist with the larger, heavier, more awkward pieces of drywall.

Large ceiling panels may have to be raised with a special lift. After the drywall is in place, installers usually attach the metal frames, also called beading, on the edges of the walls and the edges cut for windows, doorways, and vents.

Drywall finishers, also called *tapers,* seal and hide the joints where drywall panels come together and prepare the walls for painting or wallpapering. They mix a quick-drying sealing compound and spread the paste into and over the joints with a special trowel or spatula. While the paste is still wet, the finishers press paper tape over the joint and press it down. When the sealer is dry, they spread a cementing material over the tape. They blend this material into the wall to hide the joint. Sometimes finishers have to apply second or third coats of sealer to smooth out all the rough areas on the walls. Any cracks or holes and nail and screw heads in the walls or ceiling are filled with sealer.

With a final sanding of the patched areas, the walls and ceiling are ready to be painted or papered. Some finishers apply textured surfaces to walls and ceilings using trowels, brushes, rollers, or spray guns.

Most drywall installers and finishers work for painting, decorating, and drywall contractors. Some installers and finishers

SCHOOL SUBJECTS
Mathematics, Technical/shop

MINIMUM EDUCATION LEVEL
Some postsecondary training

SALARY RANGE
$21,000 to $34,000 to $60,000

OUTLOOK
Faster than the average

OTHER ARTICLES TO READ
Carpenters
Cement Masons
Construction Laborers
Floor Covering Installers
Painters and Paperhangers
Plasterers

A drywall finisher uses a hawk and a trowel to skim on a coat of mud.

operate their own contracting businesses. Others work for general contractors.

Education and Training

Most employers prefer to hire applicants with a high school diploma. Drywall installers and finishers are trained on the job. Both installers and finishers also learn to estimate job costs.

Another way to learn this trade is through apprenticeship programs. Such programs combine classroom study with on-the-job training.

Outlook

Job growth for drywall installers and finishers should be faster than the average through 2012. Increases in new construction and remodeling and high turnover in this field mean replacement workers are needed every year. In addition, drywall will continue to be used in many kinds of building construction, creating a demand for workers.

Jobs will be more plentiful in metropolitan areas where contractors have enough business to hire full-time drywall workers. Like other construction trades workers, drywall installers and finishers may go through periods of unemployment or part-time employment when the local economy is in a downturn and construction activity slows.

For More Information

It may be possible for you to visit a job site and observe installers and finishers at work. There are several home improvement and construction television programs that occasionally show the drywall installation process. Check your library for videos and books on the subject.

Arizona Carpenters Apprenticeship Web Site
http://www.azcarpenters.com

Associated Builders and Contractors
4250 N. Fairfax Drive, 9th Floor
Arlington, VA 22203-1607
703-812-2000
gotquestions@abc.org
http://www.abc.org

Association of the Wall and Ceiling Industries International
803 West Broad Street, Suite 600
Falls Church, VA 22046
703-534-8300
info@awci.org
http://www.awci.org

International Union of Painters and Allied Trades
1750 New York Avenue, NW
Washington, DC 20006
mail@iupat.org
http://www.iupat.org

# Ecologists

What Ecologists Do

Ecologists study relationships among organisms (plants and animals) and their environment, including rainfall, temperature, altitude, soil and water conditions, and pollutants. Some ecologists study an entire ecosystem, or community of plants and animals in a given habitat, such as a forest, tundra, savanna (grassland), or rain forest.

There are many complex and delicate interrelationships within an ecosystem. For example, green plants use the energy of sunlight to make carbohydrates, fats, and proteins; some animals eat these plants and acquire part of the energy of the carbohydrates, fats, and proteins; other animals eat these animals and acquire a smaller part of that energy. Cycles of photosynthesis, respiration, and nitrogen fixation continuously recycle the chemicals of life needed to support the ecosystem. Anything that disrupts these cycles, such as drought, fire, or air or water pollution, can disrupt the delicate workings of the entire ecosystem.

One primary concern of ecologists is pollution and the restoration of ecosystems that are destroyed or severely damaged because of pollution, overuse of land, or other disruptions. There are many other subspecialties within the field of ecology. Environmental planning involves studying and reporting the impact of an action, such as construction, on the environment. *Resource management ecologists* determine what resources already exist and find ways to use them wisely. *Forest ecologists* research how changes in the environment affect forests. They study the conditions that cause a certain type of tree to grow abundantly, including its light and soil requirements and its resistance to insects and disease. *Hydrogeologists* are ecologists who study the waters on or below the surface of the earth. *Geochemists* study the chemistry of the earth, including the effects of pollution on that chemistry.

Ecologists conduct studies on plants and animals both in their natural setting

---

SCHOOL SUBJECTS
Biology, Chemistry

MINIMUM EDUCATION LEVEL
Bachelor's degree

SALARY RANGE
$30,000 to $48,000 to $78,000

OUTLOOK
About as fast as average

OTHER ARTICLES TO READ
Biologists
Botanists
Chemists
Environmental Engineers
Environmental Technicians
Groundwater Professionals
Soil Conservation Technicians
Soil Scientists

and in the laboratory. They use electron microscopes, electronic instruments, computers, and other equipment in their research. Some work is done with dangerous organisms or toxic substances in the laboratory. Fieldwork may include living in remote areas under primitive conditions and may involve strenuous physical activity.

Education and Training

Earth science, biology, chemistry, English, math, and computer science classes are important preparation for a career in ecology.

You need at least a bachelor's of science degree to become an ecologist. This degree will qualify you for nonresearch jobs, such as testing or inspection. For jobs in applied research or management, a master's degree is usually necessary. In addition, a master's degree is required for advancement to administrative positions. For positions in college teaching or independent research, a doctoral degree is required.

The Ecological Society of America offers professional certification at three levels: Associate Ecologist, Ecologist, and Senior Ecologist. A candidate's certification level

Ecologists release a farm-raised alligator into a wetland area in Louisiana.

will depend on his or her level of education and professional experience.

Outlook

Environmental jobs are expected to increase about as fast as average in the next decade. Land and resource conservation jobs tend to be the scarcest, however, because of high popularity and tight budgets at the agencies that handle these issues. Ecologists with advanced degrees will find better job opportunities than those with only bachelor's degrees.

For More Information

Parks and nature preserves usually offer workshops in local plant and animal life and ecosystems. They may also offer opportunities to volunteer, especially for cleaning and maintaining trails and public access areas. Regularly visit nearby ponds, forests, or parks to observe and collect data on ecosystems. Science teachers and local park service or arboretum workers can offer guidance.

Ecological Society of America
1707 H Street, NW, Suite 400
Washington, DC 20006
202-833-8773
esahq@esa.org
http://esa.org

National Wildlife Federation
11100 Wildlife Center Drive
Reston, VA 20190-5362
703-438-6000
http://www.nwf.org

Student Conservation Association
689 River Road
PO Box 550
Charlestown, NH 03603
603-543-1700
http://www.thesca.org

Economists

SKILLS SPOTLIGHT
◆
What they do
Communicate ideas
Evaluate and manage information
Teach

Skills they need
Mathematics
Problem solving
Reasoning

What Economists Do

Everyone makes decisions on how to spend money, but *economists* do this on a grand scale. They work with companies and the government to help plan various programs and projects. Economists research how people spend their money and what goods and services are being produced.

Many economists work for businesses to help plan what products to make or services to offer and how much to charge. An economist may study such factors as how many potential customers there are in a certain area, how much they pay for a product or service, and which other companies are selling the product or service. Economists also study statistics showing how much a product costs to make and where the manufacturer should invest its profits. Economists analyze these factors and then report their findings to management officials, who use this information in future planning.

Economists collect and analyze the appropriate statistics and examine how various numbers are related. For example, an economist may find that salaries are going up and use that information to explain, in part, why prices are also increasing.

Preparing reports is another important part of economists' duties. They prepare tables and charts and write their findings in clear, direct language.

Economists usually specialize in a specific branch of their field. *Government economists* look at larger issues than those who work for private companies. Their conclusions may affect governmental policy. A *labor economist* for the government may investigate salaries paid to workers across the country and how many people are employed nationwide. They use this information to determine and report various economic trends. *International economists* study how many local goods are sold to foreign countries and how many foreign goods are bought here. They study statistics to make sure that their government is benefiting from its exchange of goods with other nations. *Financial economists* study credit, money, and other statistics and trends to help develop public

SCHOOL SUBJECTS
Business, Economics, Mathematics
MINIMUM EDUCATION LEVEL
Master's degree
SALARY RANGE
$39,000 to $69,000 to $120,000
OUTLOOK
About as fast as the average

OTHER ARTICLES TO READ
Accountants
Bank Examiners
Financial Analysts
Financial Planners
Financial Services Brokers
Insurance Underwriters

policy. *Industrial economists* study the way businesses are organized and suggest ways to use profits or other assets.

Education and Training

Courses in mathematics, English, and writing, and any available classes in economics or other social sciences, are most helpful. Computers are important in all types of statistical work, so make sure to take computer classes, particularly those that teach spreadsheet and database programs.

A bachelor's degree with a major in economics or business administration is the minimum requirement for an entry-level position such as research assistant. A master's degree, or even a Ph.D., is more commonly required for most positions as an economist. More than 90 percent of all economists have advanced degrees.

Outlook

Employment for economists is expected to grow as fast as the average in the next 10 years. Economists will find the best opportunities in private industry, especially in testing, research, and consulting. In the academic arena, economists with master's and doctoral degrees will face strong competition for desirable teaching jobs.

For More Information

Learn about business and economic trends by reading business publications, such as newspaper business sections and business news magazines. Participate in investment, economics, or political science clubs at your school. Serving as treasurer for a club can teach you about record keeping and money management.

American Economic Association
2014 Broadway, Suite 305
Nashville, TN 37203
615-322-2595
info@econlit.org
http://www.aeaweb.org

National Association for Business Economics
1233 20th Street, NW, Suite 505
Washington, DC 20036
202-463-6223
nabe@nabe.com
http://www.nabe.com

National Council on Economic Education
1140 Avenue of the Americas
New York, NY 10036
800-338-1192
info@ncee.net
http://www.ncee.net

Two economists debate the findings of a recent study.

Education Directors and Museum Teachers

What Education Directors and Museum Teachers Do

Museums and zoos are places where people go to observe exhibits with animals, art, historic objects, and collectibles. *Education directors* and *museum teachers* help these visitors learn more about what they have come to see.

Many museums and zoos focus on helping children understand more about the exhibits. In museums, children often are allowed to handle artifacts or play with objects. In zoos, children may be able to pet animals. Education directors develop special projects to help children learn more from this type of hands-on experience.

Education directors plan, develop, and administer educational programs. These include tours, lectures, classes, workshops, and performances that focus on the history, use, design, and materials of artifacts or the behavior and habitat of animals.

In large museums, an education director may supervise a staff of museum teachers and advise them in leading workshops and classes. Directors help find ways for museum teachers to present information using materials, such as egg shells or skeletons, and instruments, such as microscopes.

In addition to museum staff members, education directors may hire speakers from local colleges or universities to lead tours or discussion groups for special exhibits. Directors work with these speakers to determine the content of a particular lecture, class, or series of lectures. They prepare course outlines and other teaching aids.

Education directors and museum teachers also work with *exhibit designers* to create displays, perhaps showing the development of a moth into a butterfly or displaying plants that animals would find in their natural environment. They work with *graphic designers* to produce signs, illustrations, and brochures that reveal more about an exhibit. Signs in a gorilla exhibit, for instance, may include a map of Africa to show where gorillas live.

Most education directors at museums work in art, history, or science, but other museums have a special interest, such as woodcarvings or circuses.

Education and Training

Courses in creative writing, literature, history of world civilizations, American history, the sciences, foreign languages, art, and speech will prepare you for tasks such as interpreting collections, writing letters to school principals, designing curriculum materials, developing multicultural education, and lecturing to public audiences.

Education directors and museum teachers must have at least a bachelor's degree. A liberal arts degree is common, but a degree in one of the sciences is also acceptable.

Outlook

The employment outlook for education directors and museum teachers is expected to increase more slowly than the average through the next decade. Budget cutbacks have affected many museums and other cultural institutions, which have in turn reduced the size of their education departments. Museums in the United States have seen significant reduction in the number of visitors, which is directly related to the slowdown in the travel industry.

For More Information

Most zoos and museums have student volunteers. You may be able to help with

The education director at an art museum lectures to a group of students.

elementary school tours, organize files or audiovisual materials, or assist a lecturer in a class. The American Association of Museums publishes *Museum Careers: A Variety of Vocations.* The American Association for State and Local History publishes *Introduction to Museum Work,* which discusses the educational programs at various museums.

American Association for State and Local History
1717 Church Street
Nashville, TN 37203-2991
615-320-3203
history@aaslh.org
http://www.aaslh.org

American Association of Botanical Gardens and Arboreta
100 W 10th Street, Suite 614
Wilmington, DE 19801
302-655-7100
http://www.aabga.org

American Association of Museums
1575 Eye Street, NW, Suite 400
Washington, DC 20005
202-289-1818
http://www.aam-us.org

Elder Law Attorneys

What Elder Law Attorneys Do

Elder law attorneys are lawyers who specialize in providing legal services for the elderly and, in some cases, people with disabilities. Unlike other lawyers who deal with one field of law, such as tax lawyers, elder law attorneys often deal with several fields of law when providing services to their clients. Some of the most common elder law issues include guardianship or conservatorship, public benefits (Medicaid, Medicare, and Social Security), probate and estate planning, health and long-term care planning, and elder abuse cases.

Elder law attorneys deal with all of the legal needs of their clients. They may help one client with estate planning. They may counsel another client about planning for mental incapacity and compose an alternative decision-making document that will allow another family member, for example, to make decisions about that client's health care. They may assist another client in planning for possible long-term care needs, including nursing home care. Locat-ing the appropriate type of care, coordinating private and public resources to finance the cost of care, and working to ensure the client's right to quality care are all part of the elder law practice.

Elder law lawyers must know the law's position on a variety of issues. These issues include the following: health and long-term care planning, surrogate decision-making (that is, when the client has appointed someone, most likely a relative, to make financial or other decisions when the client is unable to), obtaining public benefits (including Medicaid, Medicare, and Social Security). In addition, elder law lawyers must be capable of handling matters related to managing diminished capacity (such as when the client can no longer think clearly), and the conservation and administration of the older person's estate (including wills, trusts, and probate). Finally, elder law attorneys must be able to recognize cases of abuse, neglect, and exploitation of an older client.

Education and Training

To become a lawyer you will need to earn a college degree and a law degree. Take a college preparatory program in high school.

To enter any law school approved by the American Bar Association, you must satisfactorily complete at least three, and usually four, years of college work and pass the Law School Admissions Test. Most full-time law degree programs take three years to complete. Upon completing law school, students usually receive the juris doctor (J.D.) degree or bachelor of laws (LL.B.) degree.

To obtain a law license, lawyers must be admitted to the bar association of the state in which they will practice.

The National Elder Law Foundation offers certification to attorneys who have met specific practicing and continuing legal education requirements in the field of elder law.

Elder law attorneys discuss a client's case.

Outlook

The demand for all lawyers is expected to grow as fast as the average through 2012. Lawyers who specialize in elder law will have the advantage of a rapidly growing elderly population, increasingly complex laws, and unprecedented health care issues.

A record number of law school graduates has created strong competition for jobs, and new attorneys, even those with an eye toward elder law specialization, will initially face stiff competition for jobs.

For More Information

To learn more about the legal profession in general, sit in on some trials at your local or state courthouse. You can go to law-related Web sites to learn more about legal terminology, current court cases, and the field of law in general. Volunteer to work with the elderly to learn about their specific needs, concerns, and opinions.

American Bar Association Service Center
541 North Fairbanks Court
Chicago, IL 60611
312-988-5522
abasvcctr@abanet.org
http://www.abanet.org

National Academy of Elder Law Attorneys Inc.
1604 North Country Club Road
Tucson, AZ 85716
520-881-4005
http://www.naela.org

National Elder Law Foundation
1604 North Country Club Road
Tucson, AZ 85716
520-881-1076
http://www.nelf.org

Electrical and Electronics Engineers

What Electrical and Electronics Engineers Do

For electrical equipment to operate properly, it needs to be designed and built by experts who understand wiring and other construction requirements. *Electrical and electronics engineers* design new products, test equipment, and solve operating problems. They also estimate the time and money it will take to build a new product and make sure budgets are met.

Electrical and electronics engineers work on all types of projects in a wide variety of fields, including acoustics, speech, and signal processing; electromagnetic compatibility; geoscience and remote sensing; lasers and electro-optics; robotics; ultrasonics, ferroelectrics, and frequency control; and automotive technology.

Some electrical engineers focus on high-power generation of electricity and how it is transmitted for use in lighting homes and powering factories. They design

and maintain communications equipment that transmits data via wire and airwaves. Some engineers work on the design and construction of power plants. Other electrical and electronics engineers are involved in the design, manufacture, and maintenance of industrial machinery that must be precisely timed and calibrated to operate in conjunction with other machines. Some engineers build the electric motors used in airplanes, cars, and other vehicles.

There are electronics engineers who specialize in broadcasting equipment at radio and television stations and others who work with smaller-scale applications, such as computers, appliances, televisions, stereos, security systems, and medical equipment.

All electrical and electronics engineers draw blueprints to show how a piece of equipment should be constructed and how it operates. They complete more detailed drawings that show how wiring should be connected. Engineers build prototypes, or samples, to test the accuracy of their plans. They write reports on all their findings and make changes when necessary. When final plans have been drawn, engineers supervise the production of parts and equipment and test it again to make sure it works properly.

Electrical and electronics engineers work with many other professionals, including other types of engineers, technicians, production workers, and administrative officials.

Education and Training

Electrical and electronics engineers need a solid background in mathematics and science and an understanding of how mathematical and scientific concepts can be used to solve technical problems. They must be skillful in making clear sketches of unfinished equipment and have the ability to explain in understandable language how complex equipment operates.

In order to become an electrical and electronics engineer, you must earn a bachelor's degree in electrical engineering, electronics engineering, or computer engineering. A degree in mathematics or science is sometimes acceptable if you also have extensive course work in engineering.

Many electrical and electronics engineers have master's degrees or Ph.D.'s. Engineers who plan to teach in colleges or do research usually are required to have a Ph.D.

Outlook

The increased use of electronic components in automobiles and increases in computer and telecommunications production require a high number of skilled engineers. There is a growing need for upgrading existing aircraft and weapons systems, which will create a demand for electrical and electronics engineers. The development of

An electrical engineering student works at a training station.

electrical and electronic goods for the consumer market is also continuing to grow.

For More Information

Join a science club at your school. Consider joining the Junior Engineering Technical Society, which provides hands-on activities and opportunities to explore scientific topics in depth. Student members can join competitions and design structures that exhibit scientific knowledge. Try building a radio or a computer central processing unit.

Institute of Electrical and Electronics Engineers
1828 L Street, NW, Suite 1202
Washington, DC 20036-5104
http://www.ieee.org

Junior Engineering Technical Society Inc.
1420 King Street, Suite 405
Alexandria, VA 22314-2794
jetsinfo@jets.org
http://www.jets.org

Michigan Technological University Summer Youth Program
Youth Programs Office
1400 Townsend Drive
Houghton, MI 49931-1295
http://www.mtu.edu

Electricians

SKILLS SPOTLIGHT

◆

What they do
Evaluate and manage information
Fix or repair technology
Select and apply tools/technology

Skills they need
Problem solving
Responsibility
Self-management

What Electricians Do

Electricians install and repair the wiring and electrical equipment that supplies light, heat, refrigeration, air conditioning, telecommunications, and other electrically powered services. Electricians work on constructing new buildings, on remodeling old ones, and on making electrical repairs in homes, offices, factories, and other businesses.

Electricians usually specialize in either construction or maintenance. Most *construction electricians* are employed by contractors or builders. Some work for large employers that need construction electricians fairly constantly, such as large industrial plants or state highway departments.

In installing wiring, construction electricians follow blueprints and specifications, or they prepare sketches showing the intended location of wiring and equipment. They bend conduit (metal pipe or tubing that holds wiring) so that it will fit snugly on the walls, floors, or beams to which it will be attached. They pull insulated wires or cables through the conduit. Electricians strip insulation from wires, splice and solder wires together, and tape or cap the ends. They attach cables and wiring to the incoming electrical service and to various fixtures and machines that use electricity. They install switches, circuit breakers, relays, transformers, grounding leads, signal devices, and other electrical components. Finally, they test the circuit to be sure that it is grounded, that the connections are properly made, and that the circuits are not overloaded.

Maintenance electricians carry out periodic inspections to find and fix problems before they occur. They check the reliability of motors, electronic controls, and telephone wiring. They make whatever repairs are necessary and change defective fuses, switches, circuit breakers, and wiring. Maintenance electricians work in manufacturing industries, such as those that produce automobiles, aircraft, ships, steel, chemicals, and industrial machinery. Some work for hospitals, municipalities, housing complexes, or shopping centers to do maintenance, repair, and sometimes installation work.

SCHOOL SUBJECTS
Mathematics, Technical/shop
MINIMUM EDUCATION LEVEL
Apprenticeship
SALARY RANGE
$25,000 to $42,000 to $69,000
OUTLOOK
Faster than the average

OTHER ARTICLES TO READ
Appliance Repairers
Electrical and Electronics Engineers
Electromechanical Technicians
Electronics Service Technicians
Elevator Installers and Repairers

An electrician reads a circuit map.

Education and Training

A high school education is the first step toward a career in this field. Most electricians agree that the best way to learn the trade is through an apprenticeship program.

Apprenticeship participants generally must be between 18 and 24 years old, and you must take tests to determine your aptitude for the trade. Most apprenticeship programs involve four years of on-the-job training in which you work for several electrical contractors engaged in different types of work.

Electronics specialists receive certification training and testing through the International Society of Certified Electronic Technicians. Some states and municipalities require that electricians be licensed.

Outlook

Employment of electricians is expected to grow faster than the average through 2012. This growth will result from an overall increase in residential and commercial construction and the increasing use of electrical and electronic devices and equipment, especially computer, telecommunications, and data-processing equipment. Electricians will be needed to upgrade old wiring and to install and maintain more extensive wiring systems as more people and businesses are choosing to rehab old buildings rather than construct new ones.

For More Information

Hobbies such as repairing radios, building electronics kits, or working with model electric trains can help develop useful skills you will need as an electrician. Join a science club that allows you to work on projects related to electricity.

Independent Electrical Contractors
4401 Ford Avenue, Suite 1100
Alexandria, VA 22302
info@ieci.org
http://www.ieci.org

International Brotherhood of Electrical Workers
900 Seventh Street, NW
Washington, DC 20001
http://www.ibew.org

International Society of Certified Electronic Technicians
3608 Pershing Avenue
Fort Worth, TX 76107-4527
info@iscet.org
http://www.iscet.org

National Electrical Contractors Association
3 Bethesda Metro Center, Suite 1100
Bethesda, MD 20814
http://www.necanet.org

# Electric Power Workers

What Electric Power Workers Do

Electric power workers make sure electricity is available whenever it is needed. Without electric power workers to guide and manage the flow of electricity, power would never reach our homes, businesses, factories, and hospitals. Electric power workers are employed in plants fueled by coal, oil, natural gas, and nuclear power.

There are several kinds of electric power workers. *Load dispatchers* give orders, usually over the phone, about how much electricity should be produced and where it should be released. By reading meters and recorders, load dispatchers know at any time how much power is flowing and where. If lines are down or need repair, load dispatchers arrange for their removal and service. Load dispatchers keep careful records of all normal and emergency situations that occur on their shifts, and they inform the proper authorities when lines or equipment need attention.

A *substation operator* controls the flow of electricity by flipping switches at the control board at one of the power company's substations. Substation operators monitor and record the board's readings and then give the data, such as the amount of electricity distributed and used, to operators at the main generating plant. These operators then connect or break the flow by pulling levers that control circuit breakers.

Line installers put up the power lines, which consist of poles, cables, and other equipment that conduct electricity from the power plant to where it will be used.

Ground helpers aid the line installers in digging the holes and then raising the poles. They also help string cables from pole to pole or from pole to building.

Trouble shooters are line workers who service transmission lines that are not working properly. Because they deal with energized lines (lines that have electricity in them), they must take extra precautions to avoid burns or electric shock.

Cable splicers do work similar to that of line installers, but with cables. Underground cables are used where raising a pole on a street corner is too difficult. Cable

---

SCHOOL SUBJECTS
Physics, Technical/shop

MINIMUM EDUCATION LEVEL
High school diploma

SALARY RANGE
$37,000 to $57,000 to $81,000

OUTLOOK
Decline

OTHER ARTICLES TO READ
Cable Television Technicians
Electromechanical Technicians
Line Installers and Cable Splicers
Mechanical Engineering Technicians

splicers work in tunnels or on cables buried in yards, under streets, or through buildings and spend most of their time in maintenance and repair work.

Education and Training

Most electric power workers are at least high school graduates who learn the trade either through on-the-job training or through an apprenticeship program. To be prepared for either type of training, class work should include mathematics, physics, and shop. You need three to seven years of work as an assistant or junior operator before you can operate a large substation, and you need seven to 10 years' experience as a substation operator before you become a load dispatcher.

An apprenticeship program includes classes in such things as blueprint reading, electrical theory, transmission theory, electrical codes, and job safety practices.

An electrical power worker wears safety gloves, a helmet, and glasses to avoid injury while wiring the power lines.

Load dispatchers and substation operators need a background that includes good training in sciences and mathematics as well as years of job experience with the company. College-level courses are desirable.

Outlook

Employment for transmission and distribution workers is expected to decline, in part because of industry deregulation and increased competition between electric light and power companies. In addition, technological improvements have made some equipment more efficient and reliable, and the use of automatic controls is reducing the need for people to monitor and regulate transmission and distribution systems.

For More Information

Physics and drafting courses are important for careers in electric power. Some power plants have visitors' centers where the public is allowed to observe some of the plant operations and to learn how electricity is generated and distributed to consumers.

Edison Electric Institute
701 Pennsylvania Avenue, NW
Washington, DC 20004-2696
202-508-5000
http://www.eei.org

International Brotherhood of Electrical Workers
900 Seventh Street NW
Washington, DC 20001
202-833-7000
http://www.ibew.org

U.S. Department of Energy
1000 Independence Avenue, SW
Washington, DC 20585
http://www.energy.gov

Electrologists

SKILLS SPOTLIGHT

◆

What they do
Evaluate and manage information
Help clients and customers
Select and apply tools/technology

Skills they need
Decision making
Responsibility
Social

What Electrologists Do

Electrologists remove unwanted hair from the skin of clients. They use an electric probe that, with repeated use, ultimately kills the hair root and prevents hair from growing back.

Electrologists usually begin their work with a personal interview with the client to understand what the client's wishes and expectations are. The electrologist explains in detail the process, possible side effects, the estimated length of sessions, the duration of treatment, and the cost. Electrologists also suggest alternate methods of hair removal that may be more cost effective or appropriate for a client's needs.

Before beginning a session, electrologists make sure that the treatment area and instruments are sterile. The first step in the treatment is the cleansing of the area of skin that will be treated with rubbing alcohol or an antiseptic. After the skin is properly cleansed, the electrologist uses a round-tipped probe to penetrate the hair follicle and the papilla, which is the organ beneath the hair root. The electrologist sets the proper amount and duration of the electrical current in advance and presses on a floor pedal to distribute the current through the probe. After the current is delivered, the hair can be lifted out with a pair of tweezers. Good visual acuity and fine motor abilities are essential.

Electrologists determine an appropriate schedule of treatments for each client. Weekly appointments may last 15, 30, 45, or even 60 minutes. The length of the individual appointments depends on both the amount of hair to be removed and the thickness and depth of the hair. Very coarse hair may take longer to treat, whereas fine hair may be permanently removed in only a few sessions.

If a patient is very sensitive to the treatments, the electrologist may set up shorter appointments or schedule more time between sessions. Some electrologists use a gold needle on sensitive clients to minimize adverse reactions, which can include itching, bumps, redness, and pustules. Most of these reactions can be treated with topical ointments and proper skin care.

SCHOOL SUBJECTS
Biology, Health

MINIMUM EDUCATION LEVEL
Some postsecondary training

SALARY RANGE
$13,000 to $19,000 to $35,000

OUTLOOK
About as fast as the average

OTHER ARTICLES TO READ
Barbers
Cosmeticians
Cosmetologists
Makeup Artists

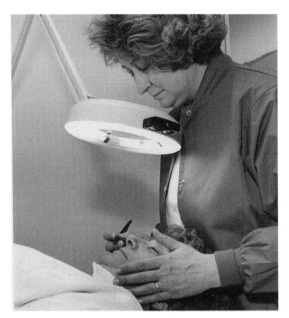

This electrologist gently removes the darker facial hair from this woman's upper lip.

A neat and professional appearance is important, so electrologists often wear uniforms or lab coats.

Education and Training

If you are interested in a career in electrology, take classes in science, anatomy and physiology, and health. Classes in communications, psychology, and business are also helpful. Good people skills are necessary.

With a high school diploma or equivalency certificate you may enroll in a trade school or professional school that offers electrolysis training. In these programs, you study microbiology, dermatology, neurology, electricity, and proper sanitation and sterilization procedures. In addition to classroom study you get practical experience under supervision. You will spend many hours learning the purpose and function of different types of equipment.

Most states require that electrologists be licensed. Licensing examinations are offered through the state health department. Licensing requirements vary from state to state.

Outlook

Employment for those in the cosmetology field, which includes electrologists, is expected to increase about as fast as the average in the next few years. Many salons, professional offices, hospitals, and clinics are offering cutting-edge technologies and services to maintain a competitive edge, which will create more jobs for electrologists.

For More Information

To find out more about the field of electrology, contact local trade schools for information. Some two-year colleges that offer course work in medical technician careers may be able to supply you with literature on programs and training in electrology. Cosmetology schools may also prove helpful in finding out about electrology.

American Electrology Association
PO Box 687
Bodega Bay, CA 94923
careeaea@electrology.com
http://www.electrology.com

International Guild of Hair Removal Specialists
1918 Bethel Road
Columbus, OH 43220
800-830-3247
http://www.ighrs.org

Society of Clinical and Medical Electrologists Inc.
2810 Crossroads Drive, Stuite 3800
Madison, WI 53718
608-443-2470
homeoffice@scmhr.org
http://www.scmhr.org

Electro-mechanical Technicians

What Electromechanical Technicians Do

Electromechanical technicians build, test, adjust, and repair such electromechanical devices as manufacturing equipment, environmental control systems, elevator controls, missile controls, and computer tape and disc drivers. An electromechanical device is one in which electronic sensors activate a mechanical operation.

Electromechanical technicians work on many different types of electromechanical devices. Technicians who work on product development and manufacturing think of new ways to use existing electromechanical equipment and try to create new types of electromechanical devices. Product development technicians help engineers and scientists conduct laboratory studies and do research on assembly and manufacturing techniques. They might assist in preparing a prototype of a new device by following blueprints and mechanical drawings.

Operating, testing, and adjusting electromechanical equipment is also an important responsibility of electromechanical technicians. For example, robot welders in automobile manufacturing plants are electromechanical devices. Technicians must constantly check and adjust robot welders so that they perform their work flawlessly. Otherwise, the cars coming off the assembly line will not be structurally sound. Technicians make sketches and rough layouts, record data, make computations, analyze results, and write reports on the testing and adjustments they complete.

Electromechanical technicians maintain and repair electromechanical devices that operate industrial machinery at manufacturing plants. Some technicians may work on environmental control systems, such as the systems that maintain the proper temperatures and humidity levels in an art museum. Other electromechanical technicians work on missile guidance systems, energy technology, medical equipment, and a large number of other fields. The types of electromechanical devices

SCHOOL SUBJECTS
Mathematics
Physics

MINIMUM EDUCATION LEVEL
Some postsecondary training

SALARY RANGE
$28,000 to $45,000 to $67,000

OUTLOOK
About as fast as the average

OTHER ARTICLES TO READ
Electrical and Electronics Engineering
Electronics Engineering Technicians
Mechanical Engineering Technicians
Mechanical Engineers

technicians work on depend on their skills, level of education, and experience.

Education and Training

To become an electromechanical technician, take as many mathematics and science courses as possible. Geometry, algebra, physics, and other lab sciences are all good choices. Also take shop classes that focus on electricity or electronics, drafting, and blueprint reading. English classes that stress speech and composition skills are also important.

Many colleges and technical institutes have training programs in electromechanical technology. These programs usually take two years to complete. They often include such courses as electricity and electronics, physics, technical graphics, digital computer fundamentals, English composition, and psychology and human relations.

Some companies require new employees to attend special training programs that take up to a year to complete. These programs teach employees the specifics of the equipment that a company uses or manufactures.

Outlook

Overall employment of engineering technicians is expected to increase about as fast as the average in the next 10 years. Employment is influenced by local and national economic conditions, so it varies according to industry and specialization. There is increasing demand for more sophisticated electrical and electronic products, which

An electromechanical technician manipulates one of many circuit boards used to operate a facility.

will create jobs for electrical and electronics engineering technicians and for electromechanical technicians.

For More Information

Join a science club at your school and work on electronics and electromechanical projects. Hobbies like automobile repair, model making, and electronic kit assembling can be helpful. Become familiar with hand and power tools and how to work with metals and plastics.

Institute of Electrical and Electronics Engineers
1828 L Street, NW, Suite 1202
Washington, DC 20036-5104
ieeeusa@ieee.org
http://www.ieee.org

Junior Engineering Technical Society Inc.
1420 King Street, Suite 405
Alexandria, VA 22314-2794
jetsinfo@jets.org
http://www.jets.org

Electroneuro-diagnostic Technologists

What Electroneurodiagnostic Technologists Do

Electroneurodiagnostic technologists, sometimes called *END technologists* or *EEG technologists,* usually work in hospitals. They run tests that measure brain damage and heart activity. An electroencephalogram, or EEG, is a test that measures brain waves. When brain waves stop, the patient is considered clinically dead. By recording brain waves and electrical activity in various parts of the body, EEG technologists provide information that helps doctors diagnose and treat patients. The information gathered is used by physicians (usually neurologists) to diagnose and determine the effects of certain diseases and injuries, including brain tumors, cerebral vascular strokes, Alzheimer's disease, epilepsy, some metabolic disorders, and brain injuries caused by accidents or infectious diseases.

First, the technologist asks about the patient's medical history to record any important information and help the patient feel comfortable with the testing process. Technologists prepare the patient for testing by applying electrodes to certain areas on the head.

Once prepared, patients are tested and the impulses of their brain or electrical activity are received and amplified by a machine. Tracings of electric activity are recorded on a moving sheet of paper or on optical disks. Technologists note any irregularities that occur due to pre-existing injuries or diseases in the patients. They do not interpret the test results but ensure that the results are accurate and the data complete. Then they determine which sections should be brought to the doctor's attention. Technologists give results to doctors, who use them in diagnosing diseases and injuries.

The role of electroneurodiagnostic technologists varies. They sometimes have to handle emergencies that occur during testing. Some technologists perform specialized procedures including sleep studies, evoked potential testing, during which the brain is tested with specific stimuli, or ambulatory testing, during which the patient is tested over a 24-hour period by a small

---

SCHOOL SUBJECTS
Biology, Physics

MINIMUM EDUCATION LEVEL
Some postsecondary training

SALARY RANGE
$21,000 to $34,000 to $57,000

OUTLOOK
Faster than the average

OTHER ARTICLES TO READ
Cardiovascular Technologists
Diagnostic Medical Sonographers
Medical Laboratory Technicians
Ophthalmic Laboratory Technicians

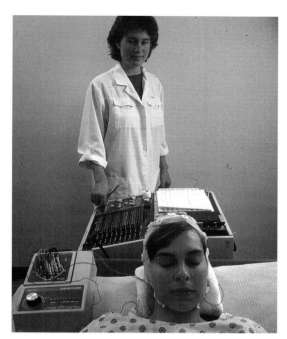

An electroneurodiagnostic technologist conducts an EEG on a patient.

recording device on the patient's side. In addition, EEG technologists have record-keeping and administrative duties. They are responsible for the maintenance of the equipment.

Education and Training

EEG technologists must have a high school diploma. Classes in mathematics and science, especially physics and chemistry, are useful. Classes in computer science are a necessity for technical professions, due to the large amounts of information that must be recorded and accessed.

EEG technologists usually are required to complete a training program. There are two types of postsecondary school training: on-the-job training and formal classroom training. Training programs usually last from one to two years, offering either a certificate or associate's degree upon completion. Courses are offered by hospitals, medical centers, and community or technical colleges.

Outlook

Employment of electroneurodiagnostic technologists is expected to grow faster than the average because of a growing and aging population that is increasing the demand for diagnostic measuring technology. Employment growth for END technologists in the area of polysomnography (to evaluate sleep and sleep disorders), long-term monitoring for epilepsy, and intraoperative monitoring will be particularly strong.

For More Information

Volunteer at a local hospital, clinic, or nursing home to learn more about working in the health care field. Join a science or computer club to work on electronics projects, or research different kinds of medical imaging.

American Board of Registration of Electroencephalographic and Evoked Potential Technologists
1904 Croydon Drive
Springfield, IL 62703
217-553-3758
http://www.abret.org

American Society of Electroneurodiagnostic Technologists
428 West 42nd Street, Suite B
Kansas City, MO 64111
816-931-1120
http://www.aset.org

Association of Polysomnographic Technology
PO Box 14861
Lenexa, KS 66285-4861
913-541-1991
http://www.aptweb.org

Electronics Engineering Technicians

What Electronics Engineering Technicians Do

Electronics engineering technicians create, assemble, install, operate, maintain, and repair electronic devices such as radios, televisions, computers, stereos, VCRs, DVD players, and pocket calculators. Some technicians work directly with scientists and engineers in product development. They build, test, and modify experimental electronics products. As part of their work, they use hand tools and small machine tools. They make complex electronic parts and components and use advanced instruments to check the results of their work. Sometimes they make suggestions to improve the performance or design of an electronic device.

An important part of a technician's job is testing a new product before it is ready to be sold. Before testing new parts and systems, technicians first study the wiring diagrams and technical manuals that accompany the products they're testing.

They learn various tests from the manuals or through special instructions they receive from engineers or other supervisors.

Technicians usually begin their tests by connecting the part or unit to a special testing piece of electronic equipment such as a signal generator, frequency meter, or spectrum analyzer. The technician reads dials on the testing device that indicate electronic characteristics such as the amount of voltage that is going through the unit. The technician then compares the results with the correct level specified in manuals. In this way, the technician can locate a problem such as a short circuit or a defective component. Then he or she can replace the wiring or component or send instructions about how to fix it to a repair or production department.

Technicians who work on product development may also become involved in estimating how much it will cost to manufacture an electronic device. This allows the sales department to determine how much to charge the consumer.

SCHOOL SUBJECTS
Computer science, Mathematics, Physics

MINIMUM EDUCATION LEVEL
High school diploma

SALARY RANGE
$17,000 to $21,000 to $41,000

OUTLOOK
Decline

OTHER ARTICLES TO READ
Biomedical Equipment Technicians
Electrical and Electronics Engineers
Electronics Service Technicians
Microelectronics Technicians
Robotics Engineers and Technicians

Waiting for the production of one circuit board, an electronics technician examines another board.

Electronics technicians may also help manufacture electronics products, write instruction manuals, and test programs. They solve production problems, make up production schedules, and collaborate with, supervise, and train production employees.

Education and Training

To prepare for a career in electronics engineering, you should take at least two years of mathematics, including geometry and algebra in high school. You also should take physics, chemistry, computer science, and English. An introductory electronics course, shop courses, and courses in mechanical drawing are also useful.

After high school, you should enroll in a two-year training program offered by a community college or technical school. These programs include courses in physics, technical mathematics, applied electron-

ics, and circuit analysis. Some companies, such as utility companies, offer on-the-job training programs to high school graduates with good science backgrounds.

Some electronics jobs require certification. Technicians working on radio transmission equipment require a license from the Federal Communications Commission. Other technicians earn voluntary certification to demonstrate a certain level of competency.

Outlook

The employment of electronics engineering technicians is expected to decline through 2012 because of increasing automation and the shift to countries with lower labor costs. As manufacturers strive to improve productivity and precision, automated machinery progressively will be used to undertake work more economically and more efficiently.

For More Information

Join electronics or radio clubs in school. Practice assembling electronic equipment with one of the commercial kits available.

Electronics Technicians Association International
5 Depot Street
Greencastle, IN 46135
http://www.eta-i.org

Institute of Electrical and Electronics Engineers Inc.
1828 L Street, NW, Suite 1202
Washington, DC 20036-5104
http://www.ieee.org

Junior Engineering Technical Society
1420 King Street, Suite 405
Alexandria, VA 22314
jetsinfo@jets.org
http://www.jets.org

Electroplating Workers

SKILLS SPOTLIGHT
◆
What they do
Evaluate and manage information
Select and apply tools/technology
Work with a team

Skills they need
Mathematics
Problem solving
Self-management

What Electroplating Workers Do

When an object is electroplated, it is covered by a layer of gold, silver, brass, or other metal. Electroplating gives objects such as car bumpers or electronics parts a hard, protective surface.

Electroplating workers study a product's specifications and decide which parts need plating, what type of plating to use, and how thickly the metal should be applied. Workers then mix the plating solution. They mathematically calculate proportions for solutions that are often caustic and dangerous. Because of the dangers, electroplaters must work carefully to be sure their calculations are accurate. The platers prepare the object for the plating process by putting it through various cleaning and rinsing baths. They may have to measure, mark, and mask off (with lacquer, rubber, or tape) parts of the object that are to be left unplated.

Next, workers place the object in tanks in order for the plating to reach the right thickness. The metal adheres to the object through an electrical process that is controlled by the plater. When the object is rinsed and dried, the plater looks for problems and checks the thickness of the metal.

Sometimes workers are designated according to the specific type of electroplating equipment they operate. For example, *barrel platers* operate a mesh barrel that is filled with objects to be plated; *production platers* operate automatic plating equipment; and *electroformers* prepare objects for plating that do not conduct electricity, such as baby shoes or books.

The exact nature of electroplating workers' jobs depends on the size of the shop in which they work. In a large shop, chemists or chemical engineers may make the major decisions. In a small shop, however, the electroplating worker is often responsible for the whole process, including ordering chemicals, preparing solutions, plating the products, and inspecting them upon completion.

SCHOOL SUBJECTS
Chemistry, Mathematics, Technical/
  shop
MINIMUM EDUCATION LEVEL
High school diploma
SALARY RANGE
$18,000 to $32,000 to $51,000
OUTLOOK
Decline

OTHER ARTICLES TO READ
Chemical Technicians
Jewelers
Metallurgical Engineers and Technicians

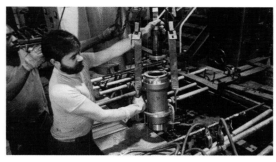
Two electroplating workers finish the surface of a chrome machine part.

Education and Training

If you are interested in becoming an electroplater, classes in mathematics, chemistry, physics, electrical shop, metal shop, and blueprint reading will be helpful.

Electroplating is best learned through a one- or two-year technical program at a community college or vocational school. Plating processes have become more complex in recent years and require more precision. Employers usually prefer to hire students who have had specialized training and technical education. Many electroplaters, however, start out as helpers with little prior training and learn the trade by working with skilled platers.

Outlook

The number of jobs in the electroplating industry is expected to decline through 2012. Although there is expected to be a greater number of electroplated items produced, automation will reduce the number of workers needed. The demand for plastic products has increased, and plastics have replaced metals in many consumer goods in recent years. There is also increasing competition from foreign manufacturers in the metals and plastics industries.

Nonetheless, every year new job openings will occur for new positions and to replace workers who transfer to other occupations. Students who have completed a technical program in electroplating have the best opportunities to find entry-level positions. Workers who can operate a variety of machines and who know the properties of metals and plastics will have better employment opportunities.

For More Information

Participate in metalworking hobbies to learn about the basic properties of metals. Ask a school counselor or teacher to arrange a tour of an electroplating facility.

American Electroplaters and Surface Finishers Society
12644 Research Parkway
Orlando, FL 32826
407-281-6441
http://www.aesf.org

National Association of Metal Finishers
21165 Whitfield Place, Suite 105
Potomac Falls, VA 20165
703-433-2522
http://www.namf.org

Elementary School Teachers

What Elementary School Teachers Do

Elementary school teachers plan lessons, teach a variety of subjects, and keep records of academic performance, behavior, and attendance for each student. Elementary school is usually defined as kindergarten through the sixth grade.

Elementary school teachers instruct approximately 20 to 30 students in the same grade. Teachers of the early grades teach basic skills in reading, writing, counting, and telling time. With older students, they lead lessons in history, geography, math, reading, and writing. In some elementary schools, there are special teachers for art, music, and physical education. Teachers use a variety of aids to instruct students, including the computer and Internet, textbooks, workbooks, magazines, newspapers, maps, charts, and posters. They sometimes use arts and crafts projects, music, science experiments, contests, and role playing.

Some elementary school teachers work in multi-age classrooms, where students in a small age range are taught together. Others teach in bilingual classrooms, where students are instructed in two languages throughout the day. Many teachers have one or more students with disabilities in their classrooms as well.

In addition to teaching, teachers have the challenge of maintaining order in the classroom, handling disciplinary problems, and resolving conflicts. They give instruction in social skills along with general school subjects. They serve as disciplinarians, establishing and enforcing rules of conduct to help students learn right from wrong.

Teachers spend a lot of time outside of the classroom planning classes; grading papers, tests, and homework assignments; preparing student reports; ordering books and supplies; preparing and making copies of printed materials for students; talking to parents; and meeting with other teachers, the principal, and school administrators.

SCHOOL SUBJECTS
English, Speech

MINIMUM EDUCATION LEVEL
Bachelor's degree

SALARY RANGE
$29,000 to $43,000 to $67,000

OUTLOOK
About as fast as the average

OTHER ARTICLES TO READ
English as Second Language Teachers
Guidance Counselors
Preschool Teachers
Secondary School Teachers
Special Education Teachers
Teacher Aides

They may have to meet with school psychologists and social workers to help students with learning difficulties and behavioral or physical problems.

Elementary school teachers may have to plan duties and schedules for teachers' aides and student teachers as well as evaluate their performance.

Most teachers are contracted to work 10 months out of the year, with a two-month vacation during the summer.

Education and Training

To be an elementary school teacher you need a well-rounded education with courses in English, math, science, history, and government.

All school teachers must be college graduates and must be certified by the state in which they want to teach. Part of their education includes several weeks as a student teacher, participating in an actual elementary school classroom under the guidance of a certified teacher. College programs in education lead to state certification.

Some states may require prospective teachers to take additional certification tests upon graduating from an education program. Students who earn a bachelor's degree in another field can take additional education courses to fulfill certification requirements.

Outlook

Employment opportunities for teachers of grades K-12 are expected to grow as fast as the average for all occupations through 2012. The demand for teachers varies widely depending on geographic area. Inner-city schools often suffer a shortage of teachers.

This elementary school teacher fingerpaints with a group of students during an art lesson.

More opportunities exist for teachers who specialize in a subject in which it is harder to attract qualified teachers, such as mathematics, science, or foreign languages.

For More Information

Look for leadership opportunities that involve working with children, such as being a camp counselor, a leader of a scout troop, or an assistant in a public park or community center. Look for opportunities to tutor younger students or coach children's athletic teams. Teach a younger sibling to read and do simple arithmetic.

American Federation of Teachers
555 New Jersey Avenue, NW
Washington, DC 20001
202-879-4400
online@aft.org
http://www.aft.org

National Education Association
1201 16th Street, NW
Washington, DC 20036
202-833-4000
http://www.nea.org

Elevator Installers and Repairers

What Elevator Installers and Repairers Do

Elevator installers and repairers, also called *elevator constructors* or *mechanics,* assemble and install elevators, escalators, and dumbwaiters. Today's elevators are usually electronically controlled. They typically have computerized controls called microprocessors, which are programmed to determine how many people are using the elevator at any given time and to send elevators up and down when and where they are needed. Because of these sophisticated devices, elevator installers have a strong mechanical ability and a thorough understanding of electronics and hydraulics.

Elevator installers begin a job by first studying the blueprints of the elevator's planned location in a building to determine where everything is going to fit. The next step is to direct a crew in installing the guide rails of the car along the walls of the elevator shaft. To set up the elevator's electrical system, electrical conduit is run along the shaft's walls from one floor to the next, and then plastic-covered electrical wire is threaded through it. After installing all the electrical components on each floor and in the control panel, installers assemble the steel frame of the elevator car at the bottom of the shaft and connect the platform, walls and door.

In elevators operated by cable, mechanics install an electrically powered spool that winds a heavy steel cable connecting the car to a counterweight. When the car moves up, the counterweight moves down, and vice versa. Other elevators function on a hydraulic pumping system, which has a cylinder that pushes the car up from underneath instead of a cable that pulls it up from above. New technology also is becoming available to run elevators using magnetic fields. Regardless of the type of elevator being installed, the entire system has to be checked, adjusted, and tested before it can be used by the public.

Elevator mechanics also install escalators. To do this, they put in the steel framework, the electrically powered stairs, and

SCHOOL SUBJECTS
Mathematics, Technical/shop

MINIMUM EDUCATION LEVEL
Apprenticeship

SALARY RANGE
$35,000 to $56,000 to $77,000

OUTLOOK
About as fast as the average

OTHER ARTICLES TO READ
Construction Laborers
Electrical and Electronics Engineers
Electricians
Electromechanical Technicians
Electronics Engineering Technicians

An elevator installer places guide rails in a new elevator shaft.

the large track on which the stairs rotate. Then they attach the motors and electrical wiring. Increasingly, installers are working on APMs, or automated people-movers, the moving sidewalks often seen at airports.

Elevator repairers inspect and adjust elevators that are already installed. They fix doors that come off their tracks and replace electrical motors, hydraulic pumps, and control panels. They check all cables for wear.

Elevator installers and repairers use a variety of tools and machinery, including hand tools, power tools, welding machines, cutting torches, rigging equipment, and testing meters and gauges.

Education and Training

Elevator installers and repairers complete a six-month, on-the-job training program at an elevator factory. After completing this program, trainees work for 60 days on probation, and after six more months they become helpers. Helpers become fully qualified journeyman installers within five years of combined classroom and practical on-site study and after passing an examination.

Trainees also must take classes in electricity and electronics, if they have not already studied these subjects. Even experienced installers continue to receive training from their employers to keep up with new technological developments.

Outlook

Employment growth for elevator installers and repairers is expected to be about as fast as the average, although many factors will influence this growth rate. This occupation is small in terms of numbers of installers, and job turnover in this field is relatively low because of high wages.

For More Information

Courses in machine shop and blueprint reading are good preparation for this career. Any experience in construction is helpful.

International Union of Elevator Constructors
5565 Sterret Place, Suite 310
Columbia, MD 21044
http://www.iuec.org

National Association of Elevator Contractors
1298 Wellbrook Circle, Suite A
Conyers, GA 30012
800-900-6232
http://www.naec.org

National Elevator Industry Educational Program
11 Larsen Way
Attleboro Falls, MA 02763-1068
508-699-2200
http://www.neiep.org

Emergency Medical Technicians

What Emergency Medical Technicians Do

Emergency medical technicians, or *EMTs,* drive in ambulances or fly in helicopters to the scene of accidents or emergencies to care for ill or injured people. They try to rapidly identify the nature of the emergency, stabilize the patient's condition, and start proper medical procedures at the scene.

EMTs often work in two-person teams. They are able to get to an emergency scene in any part of their geographic area quickly and safely. They are familiar with the roads and any special conditions affecting the choice of route, such as traffic, weather-related problems, and road construction.

EMTs are often the first qualified personnel to arrive on the scene, so they must make the initial evaluation of the medical problem. They look for medical identification emblems and other clues that indicate allergies, diabetes, epilepsy, or other conditions that may affect decisions about emergency treatment. EMTs might ask bystanders or family members for more information.

Once they have evaluated the situation, EMTs administer emergency treatment in accordance with specific instructions received over the radio from a physician. For example, they may have to open breathing passages, perform cardiac resuscitation, treat shock, or restrain emotionally disturbed patients.

People who must be transported to the hospital are put on stretchers or backboards, lifted into the ambulance, and secured for the ride. The receiving hospital's emergency department is informed by radio of the number of persons being transported and the details of the medical problems. During the ride, EMTs continue to monitor the patients and administer care as directed by the medical professional with whom they are maintaining radio contact.

Once at the hospital, EMTs help the staff bring the patients into the emergency

SCHOOL SUBJECTS
Biology, Health

MINIMUM EDUCATION LEVEL
Some postsecondary training

SALARY RANGE
$16,000 to $24,000 to $42,000

OUTLOOK
Faster than the average

OTHER ARTICLES TO READ
Firefighters
Licensed Practical Nurses
Medical Assistants
Nurse Assistants
Nurses
Physician Assistants
Physicians

An emergency medical technician inventories lifesaving equipment.

department and may assist with the first steps of in-hospital care. They supply whatever information they can, verbally and in writing, for hospital records.

Education and Training

To enter training to be an EMT you must be a high school graduate, be at least 18 years old, and have a driver's license. Many hospitals, colleges, and police and fire departments offer the basic EMT training course. The federal government requires that all EMTs pass this basic training course, which teaches you how to deal with common medical emergencies.

The National Registry of Emergency Medical Technicians (NREMT) sets standards for EMTs across the country. All EMTs who meet these standards are listed, or registered, with the NREMT. To be listed on this registry, you must finish the basic training program, have six months' work experience, and pass both a written and a practical test proving you can handle medical emergencies.

All states require EMTs to earn state certification by passing a state exam or passing the basic NREMT registration requirements.

Outlook

Overall, employment of EMTs is expected to grow faster than the average for all occupations through 2012. However, the outlook for paid EMTs depends partly on the community in which they work. In larger communities, the employment outlook should remain favorable, as volunteer services are being phased out and replaced by well-equipped emergency services operated by salaried EMTs. Smaller communities may not be able to support the level of emergency medical services that they would otherwise like to, and the employment prospects for EMTs may remain limited.

For More Information

Any health care experience is valuable for exploring this career, such as part-time, summer, or volunteer work in a hospital, clinic, or nursing home. You may also be able to take a first-aid class or training in cardiopulmonary resuscitation.

National Association of Emergency Medical Technicians
408 Monroe Street
Clinton, MS 39056-4210
info@naemt.org
http://www.naemt.org

National Registry of Emergency Medical Technicians
Rocco V. Morando Building
PO Box 29233
6610 Busch Boulevard
Columbus, OH 43229
http://www.nremt.org

Emergency Nurses

What Emergency Nurses Do

Emergency nurses provide highly skilled direct patient care to those who need emergency treatment for an illness or injury. Emergency nurses incorporate all the specialties of nursing.

The main responsibility of emergency nurses is to provide highly skilled emergency medical care for patients. Although emergency nursing is its own nursing specialty, it incorporates almost every other nursing specialty in the profession. Emergency nurses deal with pregnant women, newborn babies, patients with cancer, children, accident victims, AIDS patients, patients with Alzheimer's, the elderly, cardiac arrest patients, and psychologically disturbed and violent people.

When a patient enters the emergency facility, the nurses must first assess the patient and determine the severity of the illness or injury. This includes a quick preliminary diagnosis and assessment of the patient's overall condition. They talk to the patient and family. They also record vital signs and observe the patient's symptoms or check for injuries that may not be readily visible.

Emergency nurses must prioritize their patients' needs, especially if it is a triage situation, such as a disaster or accident involving a number of injured people. They must be able to stabilize the patient; prepare the patient for emergency testing, laboratory procedures, or surgery; and perform resuscitation, if necessary. In many instances, the nurse will have to perform initial treatment and use high-tech medical equipment until a doctor can see the patient.

In addition, they must be a good team player, working with other medical, administrative, and law enforcement personnel in what can become a very tense and emotional situation.

Often emergency nurses must be patient advocates, meaning that they must help the patient receive the best possible care and respect the patient's wishes regarding

SCHOOL SUBJECTS
Biology, Chemistry

MINIMUM EDUCATION LEVEL
Some postsecondary training

SALARY RANGE
$37,000 to $52,000 to $75,000

OUTLOOK
Faster than the average

OTHER ARTICLES TO READ
Emergency Medical Technicians
Nurse Anesthetists
Nurse Assistants
Nurse Practitioners
Nurse-Midwives
Nurses
Physician Assistants
Physicians

treatment. Nurses must be in touch with the family during the emergency crisis and help them deal with their emotions and fears.

Emergency nurses must also act as educators. This may include showing patients how to care for their wounds or injuries or recommending lifestyle changes, if necessary, to adapt to their conditions or plans of treatment.

Education and Training

Emergency nurses must first become registered nurses by completing one of the three kinds of postsecondary educational programs and passing the licensing examination. Entry-level requirements to become an emergency nurse depend on the state, the institution, its size, who it serves, and the availability of nurses in that specialty and geographical region. Usually nurses must have some nursing experience before entering the emergency-nursing field. Some institutions may require certification as an emergency room nurse.

Administrative and supervisory positions in the nursing field go to nurses who have earned at least the bachelor of science degree in nursing and several years of experience in the field.

Outlook

Job opportunities for all registered nurses, including emergency nurses, are expected to grow faster than the average through 2012. This growth will be driven by technological advances in patient care, which allow a greater number of patients to be treated. Furthermore, as millions of uninsured Americans continue to use hospital emergency rooms as the primary health

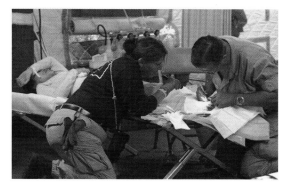

An emergency nurse assists a doctor removing shards of metal from a woman's leg during Hurricane Wilma.

care treatment facility, the demand for additional emergency nurses become very high. In addition, thousands of job openings are expected to occur because experienced older nurses are leaving the occupation. Finally, the demand for emergency nurses in nursing homes is expected to rise rapidly to meet the increases in the number of elderly in long-term care facilities.

For More Information

Volunteer at a local hospital or nursing home to interact with patients and to talk to nursing professionals on the job. Observe registered nurses at work and ask how they got started in nursing.

American Association of Colleges of Nursing
One Dupont Circle, NW, Suite 530
Washington, DC 20036
202-463-6930
info@aacn.nche.edu
http://www.aacn.nche.edu

Emergency Nurses Association
915 Lee Street
Des Plaines, IL 60016-6569
800-243-8362
enainfo@ena.org
http://www.ena.org

Endocrinologists

SKILLS SPOTLIGHT

◆

What they do
Communicate ideas
Evaluate and manage information
Help clients and customers

Skills they need
Decision making
Problem solving
Reasoning

What Endocrinologists Do

Endocrinologists are medical doctors who specialize in the treatment of disorders of the endocrine system. The endocrine system is a network of glands in the body that secrete hormones into the bloodstream. Among other things, hormones control growth, reproduction, metabolism, and blood sugar levels. Although endocrinologists may be nurses, physiologists, research scientists, and educators (to name just a few), this article will focus on endocrinologists as a physician specialty.

When the body has trouble controlling hormone levels, an individual can suffer from a variety of problems, including thyroid disease, infertility, cholesterol disorders, glandular cancers, and diabetes, to name just a few.

Endocrinologists are trained to help patients maintain the natural balance of hormones in their bodies. After diagnosing a patient, an endocrinologist might prescribe a hormone supplement or other medication; recommend changes to a patient's diet, exercise, or other habits; or refer the patient to specialists for other types of medical treatments, including surgery. Most endocrinologists are internists, obstetricians/gynecologists, or pediatricians who have completed a residency and fellowship in endocrinology. *Pediatric endocrinologists* treat disorders in growth and sexual development, as well as diseases such as diabetes and hypo- and hyperthyroidism. Pediatric endocrinologists work with patients ranging in age from infancy to adolescence. *Reproductive endocrinologists* treat patients dealing with conditions such as infertility, impotence, and problems related to menstruation and menopause. Some other areas of endocrinology specialization are diabetes, hypertension, weight disorders, and certain types of glandular cancers.

Endocrinology is a laboratory-oriented medical specialty, meaning that the diagnosis and treatment of endocrine disorders is heavily dependent on laboratory testing and expert analysis of laboratory results. Endocrinologists must also be able to distinguish disease from human variation. For example, an endocrinologist may have to

SCHOOL SUBJECTS
Biology, Health
MINIMUM EDUCATION LEVEL
Medical degree
SALARY RANGE
$43,000 to $140,000 to $146,000
OUTLOOK
About as fast as the average

OTHER ARTICLES TO READ
Biologists
Clinical Nurse Specialists
Genetic Scientists
Nurses
Pediatricians
Physicians

This endocrinologist performs a liver analysis and a hemochromatosis screening using an atomic absorption spectrophotometer.

determine whether a child of below-average height is suffering from a hormonal imbalance.

As with other types of physicians, endocrinologists' work is built around patient care. Endocrine disorders are often lifelong conditions, so endocrinologists form longstanding relationships with many patients as they manage their treatment.

Education and Training

You can prepare for a career in endocrinology by taking courses in laboratory sciences such as biology, chemistry, and physics. Courses in algebra, trigonometry, geometry, and computer science will also be crucial for future laboratory work. Courses in English will foster good communication skills.

Endocrinologists must complete a bachelor's degree, usually in biology, chemistry, or a premedical program. They then must earn a medical (M.D. or D.O.) degree, which requires four years of medical school. Then, endocrinologists must complete a minimum of four years in a specialized residency program at a teaching hospital.

After completing a residency in internal medicine, obstetrics and gynecology, or pediatrics, a specialist in endocrinology must pursue a specialized internship or fellowship in the field, usually lasting an additional three to four years.

Outlook

The employment of physicians in almost all fields is expected to grow as fast as the average for all occupations through 2012. Endocrinologists are more frequently becoming the primary care physicians of patients with lifelong disorders such as diabetes and thyroid conditions. Since many of these conditions are on the rise because of an aging population and other societal trends, endocrinologists should be in strong demand in the coming decade.

For More Information

Ask a parent or teacher to arrange a job shadowing day with an endocrinologist or medical scientist who works in a hospital, a medical research facility, or a physician's office. Examine the following Web sites to learn more about medical education and the responsibilities of endocrinologists.

American Association of Clinical Endocrinologists
1000 Riverside Avenue, Suite 205
Jacksonville, FL 32204
904-353-7878
http://www.aace.com

American Medical Association
515 North State Street
Chicago, IL 60610
800-621-8335
http://www.ama-assn.org

Endodontists

What Endodontists Do

Endodontists are dentists who specialize in diagnosing and treating diseases of the dental pulp, which consists of nerves, blood vessels, and other cells inside the tooth's root. The primary treatment they provide is the root canal. This treatment involves removal of the pulp from within the root canal, followed by filling of the root canal. Often, endodontic treatment is the only way to save a tooth that would otherwise have to be pulled.

Endodontists take X rays of affected teeth to determine what is causing the pain. They also conduct tests that show if the tooth pulp is still vital, or "alive," by evaluating the tooth's response to temperature changes, electrical stimulation, and tapping.

When performing a root canal, the endodontist anesthetizes the tooth area and drills a hole in the tooth to gain access to the pulp chamber. Using small instruments called files, the endodontist cleans and shapes the root canal, removing the pulpal tissue. After the canal has been disinfected, it is obturated, or filled, with substances such as gutta-percha (a tough plastic substance). Obturation is usually performed at a later appointment. The obturated tooth is then fitted with a crown.

In some cases, endodontic surgery is required. The endodontist cuts through the gum surgically to expose the diseased root and surrounding bone. A portion of the root may be removed surgically.

While dentists frequently perform routine root canal treatment, endodontists are better equipped to handle more complex cases, such as those involving extra tooth roots, oddly shaped root canals, or calcification. An endodontic specialist may also be the best professional to treat patients who have serious medical conditions and need root canal treatment. Endodontists also treat patients with dental injuries such as oral trauma, cracked or broken teeth, teeth that have been twisted in the socket, and teeth that have been knocked out.

Education and Training

Biology, chemistry, and health classes are good preparation for any career in dentistry.

SCHOOL SUBJECTS
Chemistry, Health

MINIMUM EDUCATION LEVEL
Medical degree

SALARY RANGE
$53,000 to $120,000 to $146,000

OUTLOOK
More slowly than the average

OTHER ARTICLES TO READ
Dental Assistants
Dental Hygienists
Dentists
Orthodontists
Physicians

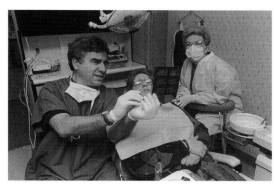
An endodontist working with a dental assistant shows his patient X rays of her teeth.

To enter dental school, you need college course work in the sciences, a bachelor's degree, and a good score on the Dental Admissions Test. After completing four years of dental school, dentists who want to specialize in endodontics attend a two- to three-year graduate training program.

Before entering practice, dentists must pass a licensing examination. In 17 states, endodontists must obtain a separate specialty license. Qualified candidates may also seek certification by the American Board of Endodontics.

Endodontists, more than most dentists, must have superb hand-eye coordination and the ability to do finely detailed work.

Outlook

Employment in dentistry is expected to grow more slowly than the average for all occupations. Most jobs will arise from the need to replace endodontists who retire or leave the occupation. As long as people place a priority on retaining their teeth, endodontists' services will continue to be in demand. The longer life spans of Americans and increasing rates of tooth retention mean that there will be more teeth that require treatment in the future. The emergency nature of many endodontic cases also keeps the demand steady.

Endodontists have to keep up with new tools and technology, such as digital radiography, nickel-titanium files, and operating microscopes that allow them to see better inside the tiny root canal.

For More Information

You can develop good manual dexterity through sculpting or metalworking or any hobby that requires the use of fine hand and power tools. Consider volunteering in any medical environment to get experience in a health care setting.

American Association of Endodontists
211 East Chicago Avenue, Suite 1100
Chicago, IL 60611-2691
Tel: 800-872-3636
info@aae.org
http://www.aae.org

American Dental Association
211 East Chicago Avenue
Chicago, IL 60611
312-440-2500
publicinfo@ada.org
http://www.ada.org

Energy Conservation and Use Technicians

What Energy Conservation and Use Technicians Do

Energy conservation and use technicians study how machines in factories, stores, and offices use energy and develop ways to use that energy more effectively. Working under the supervision of engineers or other professionals, they conduct research, perform tests, and repair or replace machines as necessary. Technicians work in a wide variety of locations, including nuclear power plants, research laboratories, and construction companies.

There are four areas in which energy conservation technicians' work: energy research and development, energy production, energy use, and energy conservation. Those in research and development often work for the military or another government agency, designing, building, and operating new laboratory experiments for a physicist,

chemist, or engineer. Technicians in energy production often work for power plants, developing and operating systems for converting fuel as efficiently as possible into electricity.

In the field of energy use, a technician might be hired to make heavy industrial equipment work more efficiently. In addition, a technician involved in energy conservation might study how a building such as a hotel could use energy more efficiently. Technicians also read blueprints and other sketches to decide if an improved design might increase energy efficiency.

In all these categories, technicians perform tests and measurements on equipment. After running tests and measurements, the technician usually prepares a report and discusses the results with management officials. Then, technicians may make recommendations, but managers make any final decisions about what actions should be taken. A manager or supervising engineer might ask the technician to run further tests

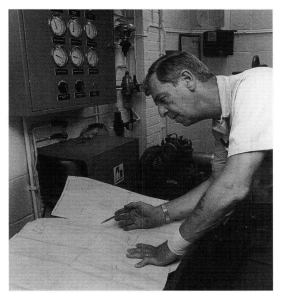

This energy conservation specialist is studying building plans for a boiler system.

and present additional findings. After a final decision is made, technicians team up with other workers to see that any necessary corrections are made.

Education and Training

The best way to enter this career is to complete a two-year training program at a community college or technical school. The program might be called energy conservation and use technology, or it may be called electric power maintenance, general engineering technology, or something similar. To be accepted into such a program, you should be a high school graduate with course work in mathematics, physics, and chemistry. Other helpful courses are ecology, computers, and mechanical or architectural drafting.

Energy conservation and use technicians should have a solid background in how machines operate, be able to read blueprints and sketches, and be able to follow instructions from supervisors. You also need to be good at mathematics and study the physical sciences. The ability to describe problems in technical language for engineers and in clearer terms for people outside the profession is also a necessity.

Outlook

Since energy use constitutes a major expense for industry, commerce, government, institutions, and private citizens, the demand for energy conservation technicians is likely to remain strong. However, employment is influenced by local and national economic conditions.

For More Information

Utility companies exist in almost every city. Energy specialists also work for large hospitals, office buildings, hotels, universities, and manufacturing plants. Contact these employers of energy technicians to learn about opportunities for volunteer, part-time, or summer work.

American Petroleum Institute
1220 L Street, NW
Washington, DC 20005-4070
202-682-8000
http://www.api.org

Association of Energy Engineers
4025 Pleasantdale Road, Suite 420
Atlanta, GA 30340
770-447-5083
http://www.aeecenter.org

National Institute for Certification in Engineering Technologies
1420 King Street
Alexandria, VA 22314-2794
888-476-4238
http://www.nicet.org

English as a Second Language Teachers

SKILLS SPOTLIGHT

◆

What they do
Communicate ideas
Help clients and customers
Teach

Skills they need
Reading/writing
Self-management
Speaking/listening

What English as a Second Language Teachers Do

English as a Second Language (ESL) teachers specialize in teaching people of all ages the English language. Their students are immigrants, refugees, children of foreign-born parents, and children who may be living in a home where English is not spoken as the primary language.

ESL teachers teach English usage, pronunciation, and grammar to help their students develop reading, writing, and speaking skills. They use classroom methods, which may include games, videos, computers, field trips, and role-playing, and other activities to teach conversation skills, telephone skills, the art of listening, and the idioms of the English language. Like other teachers, ESL teachers in public schools prepare lesson plans and exams, keep student records, and fulfill other assignments as required by the school system.

Many ESL teachers teach adults in basic education programs offered at community colleges, vocational schools, community centers, libraries, churches, and immigrant-assistance centers. Teaching adults requires skills that are different from those required to teach young people. Frequently, adults are not comfortable being back in a learning environment, so teachers may have to help them develop study habits and regain their confidence in the classroom. In addition, many adult students have jobs and may have families to care for, so teachers must be aware of the other commitments students might have and be able to adjust their teaching methods and expectations.

ESL instructors might be hired by a company to provide instruction to its workers as a part of the company's employee training or employee assistance programs, or simply as a courtesy to its workers.

Many communities have a strong networking system that involves churches, schools, health providers, resettlement

SCHOOL SUBJECTS
English, Foreign language, Speech

MINIMUM EDUCATION LEVEL
Bachelor's degree

SALARY RANGE
$27,000 to $48,000 to $82,000

OUTLOOK
Faster than the average

OTHER ARTICLES TO READ
Adult and Vocational Education Teachers
Cultural Advisers
Elementary School Teachers
Interpreters and Translators
Secondary School Teachers

programs, and other groups. ESL instructors may get involved with these groups and make visits to the students' homes to meet their families. They sometimes work with translators to communicate with the families and students. Some school systems and community programs also use translators to help the families communicate with medical providers, social workers, and government officials. ESL instructors also find many opportunities all over the world teaching English as a foreign language.

Education and Training

If you plan to teach in public school, you must earn a bachelor's degree and a teaching certificate. Teaching certificate requirements vary by state, and 23 states require that teachers placed in ESL classrooms must be certified in ESL. There are a few college programs that offer a major in ESL education. Most schools offer a major in education with a concentration in ESL as a subject area.

ESL teachers of adult students do not need an education degree or a license. There are a variety of training programs available for ESL teachers of adults. These programs usually last from four to 12 weeks, and upon successful completion, a diploma or certificate is awarded.

Outlook

There will be a continuing need for ESL teachers of adults through the next decade because of the increasing number of immigrants and other non-English speakers entering this country. Jobs will be available in the school system, community and social service agencies, and community colleges.

An ESL teacher listens as one of her students reads a presentation aloud.

For More Information

Volunteer to help with any assistance, relocation, or referral programs that your community or church might have for immigrants or refugees.

National Center for ESL Literacy Education
4646 40th Street, NW
Washington, DC 20016-1859
http://www.cal.org/ncle

National Education Association
1201 16th Street, NW
Washington, DC 20036
http://www.nea.org

Teachers of English to Speakers of Other Languages Inc.
700 South Washington Street, Suite 200
Alexandria, VA 22314
http://www.tesol.org

Environmental Engineers

What Environmental Engineers Do

Environmental engineers play an important role in helping control waste created by people in industries and municipalities. Waste includes wastewater, solid waste (garbage), hazardous waste (like radioactive waste), and air pollution.

Environmental engineers plan sewage systems, design manufacturing plant emissions systems, or develop plans for landfill sites. Scientists help decide how to break down the waste, but engineers figure out how the system will work, where the pipes will go, how the waste will flow through the system, and what equipment to use.

Environmental engineers work in the environmental departments of private industrial companies, for the Environmental Protection Agency (EPA), or for engineering consulting firms.

Environmental engineers who work for a private industrial company help make sure the company complies with environmental laws. They inspect current systems to make sure they are up to code, or they

design new waste systems for the company. For example, engineers might plan a system to move wastewater from the manufacturing process area to a treatment area, and then to a discharge site (a place where the treated wastewater can be pumped out). They write reports explaining the design. They also might file forms with the government to prove that the company is complying with the laws.

Environmental engineers working for the EPA might not actually design the waste treatment systems themselves, but they know how such systems are designed and built. If there is a pollution problem in their area, they need to figure out if a waste control system is causing the problem and what might have gone wrong. They have the authority to enforce government regulations and issue citations to offending companies.

Environmental engineers working for engineering consulting firms work on many different types of problems. Consulting firms are independent companies that

SCHOOL SUBJECTS
Mathematics, Physics

MINIMUM EDUCATION LEVEL
Bachelor's degree

SALARY RANGE
$39,000 to $61,000 to $92,000

OUTLOOK
Much faster than the average

OTHER ARTICLES TO READ
Air Quality Engineers
Ecologists
Environmental Technicians
Groundwater Professionals
Hazardous Waste Management Technicians
Renewable Energy Workers
Soil Scientists

help others comply with environmental laws. Applying engineering expertise, they design and build waste control systems for their clients. They also deal with the EPA on behalf of their clients, filling out the necessary forms and checking to see what requirements must be met.

Education and Training

To become an environmental engineer, a college degree is necessary. About 20 colleges offer a bachelor's degree in environmental engineering. Another option is to earn a degree in another type of engineering, such as civil, industrial, or mechanical engineering, with additional courses in environmental engineering. It is a good idea to take advantage of any worksite experience or internships offered through your college.

If your work as an engineer affects public health, safety, or property, you must register with the state. You must have a degree from an accredited engineering program. A few years after you have started your career, you also must pass an exam covering engineering practice.

Outlook

There will be much faster-than-average employment growth for environmental engineers through 2012. Engineers will be needed to clean up existing hazards and help companies comply with government regulations. The shift toward prevention of problems and protecting public health should create job opportunities.

For More Information

Join the local chapter of a nonprofit environmental organization, where you can learn about the particular waste problems

Environmental engineers review plans for new construction.

in your area. Participate in local campaigns to locate environmental problems and solve them.

American Academy of Environmental Engineers
130 Holiday Court, Suite 100
Annapolis, MD 21401
410-266-3311
http://www.aaee.net

Environmental Careers Organization
30 Winter Street, 6th Floor
Boston, MA 02108
617-426-4375
http://www.eco.org

Junior Engineering Technical Society, Inc.
1420 King Street, Suite 405
Alexandria, VA 22314-2794
703-548-5387
jetsinfo@jets.org
http://www.jets.org

National Association of Environmental Professionals
PO Box 2086
Bowie, MD 20718
888-251-9902
http://www.naep.org

Environmental Technicians

SKILLS SPOTLIGHT

◆

What they do
Evaluate and manage information
Help clients and customers
Select and apply tools and technology

Skills they need
Decision making
Problem solving
Reasoning

What Environmental Technicians Do

Environmental technicians, also known as *pollution control technicians,* obtain samples and conduct tests to collect data on environmental conditions. Their research is used by engineers, scientists, and others who help clean up, monitor, control, and prevent pollution.

Environmental technicians usually specialize in water pollution, air pollution, or soil pollution. *Water pollution technicians* monitor both industrial and residential discharge, such as from wastewater treatment plants. They collect samples from lakes, streams, rivers, groundwater (the water under the earth), industrial or municipal wastewater, or other sources. They bring samples to labs, where they perform chemical and other tests. If the samples contain harmful substances, remedial (cleanup) actions will need to be taken. These technicians also perform field tests, such as checking the pH, oxygen, and nitrate level of surface waters. Some technicians specialize in groundwater,

ocean water, or other types of natural waters. *Estuarine resource technicians,* for example, specialize in coastal waters where fresh water and salt water come together. These waters support a wide variety of plant and animal life that are vulnerable to destructive pollution from adjoining industries, cities and towns, and other sources.

Air pollution technicians collect and test air samples (for example, from chimneys of industrial manufacturing plants), record data on atmospheric conditions (such as determining levels of airborne substances from auto or industrial emissions), and supply data to scientists and engineers for further testing and analysis. In labs, air pollution technicians help test air samples or re-create contaminants. They may use atomic absorption spectrophotometers, flame photometers, gas chromatographs, and other instruments for analyzing samples. In the field, air pollution technicians use rooftop sampling devices or operate mobile monitoring units or stationary trailers equipped with automatic testing systems.

SCHOOL SUBJECTS
Biology, Chemistry

MINIMUM EDUCATION LEVEL
Some postsecondary training

SALARY RANGE
$23,000 to $37,000 to $57,000

OUTLOOK
About as fast as the average

OTHER ARTICLES TO READ
City Planners
Ecologists
Environmental Engineers
Hazardous Waste Management Technicians
Recycling Coordinators
Renewable Energy Workers

Technicians set up and maintain the sampling devices, replenish the chemicals used in tests, replace worn parts, calibrate instruments, and record results.

Soil or land pollution technicians collect soil, silt, or mud samples and check them for contamination. Soil can become contaminated when polluted water seeps into the earth, such as when liquid waste leaks from a landfill or other source into surrounding ground.

Noise pollution technicians use rooftop devices and mobile units to take readings and collect data on noise levels of factories, highways, airports, and other locations in order to determine noise exposure levels for workers or the public. Some test noise levels of construction equipment, chain saws, snow blowers, lawn mowers, or other equipment.

Education and Training

For some technician positions, you need at least a high school degree and employer training. As environmental work becomes more technical and complex, more positions require an associate's degree. Many community colleges have programs for environmental technicians, such as environmental engineering technologies, pollution control technologies, conservation, and ecology.

Outlook

Demand for environmental technicians is expected to increase about as fast as the average through 2012. Environmental technicians will be needed to regulate waste products; collect air, water, and soil samples for measuring levels of pollutants; monitor compliance with environmental regulations; and clean up contaminated sites.

An air pollution technician collects air quality readings from a rooftop sampling device.

For More Information

Visit your library and read technical and general-interest publications on environmental science. School science clubs, local community groups, and naturalist clubs may give you some experience. Most schools have recycling programs in which you can participate.

Air and Waste Management Association
420 Fort Duquesne Boulevard
One Gateway Center, Third Floor
Pittsburgh, PA 15222
412-232-3444
info@awma.org
http://www.awma.org

Environmental Protection Agency
Ariel Rios Building
1200 Pennsylvania Avenue, NW
Washington, DC 20460
202-260-2090
http://www.epa.gov

National Ground Water Association
601 Dempsey Road
Westerville, OH 43081-8978
800-551-7379
ngwa@ngwa.org
http://www.ngwa.org

Epidemiologists

What Epidemiologists Do

Epidemiologists study the cause, spread, and control of diseases that affect groups of people or communities. Some epidemiologists focus on infectious diseases. Others focus on noninfectious diseases, including heart disease, lung cancer, breast cancer, and ulcers.

Epidemiologists use research, statistical analysis, field investigations, and laboratory techniques to try to figure out the cause of a disease, how it spreads, and how to prevent and control it. They measure the location and frequency of an outbreak of a disease. Then, they analyze this statistical information in relation to the characteristics of populations and environments. Many epidemiologists work on developing new ways or refining old ways of measuring and evaluating incidence of disease.

Epidemiologists' work is important to the medical community and to public health officials, who use their information to determine public health policies. Epidemiologists often develop and recommend public health policies themselves using the research they have collected.

The field of epidemiology is complex and there are several specialties. *Infectious disease epidemiologists* focus on diseases caused by bacteria and viruses, such as AIDS, chicken pox, rabies, meningitis, and West Nile virus. *Chronic disease epidemiologists* study noninfectious diseases, such as diabetes, heart disease, lung cancer, breast cancer, and ulcers. Some epidemiologists study rising teenage suicide rates and murders by guns because they are considered epidemics.

Environmental epidemiologists study connections between environmental exposure and disease. They have linked radon with lung cancer and found that interior house paint can cause lead poisoning in children.

Each state has its own head epidemiologist, who is usually part of the state's public health service. These state epidemiologists work closely with the U.S. Centers for Disease Control and Prevention (CDC) in Atlanta to report certain diseases in their populations to the CDC on a regular basis.

SCHOOL SUBJECTS
Biology, Health

MINIMUM EDUCATION LEVEL
Master's degree

SALARY RANGE
$35,000 to $54,000 to $83,000

OUTLOOK
Faster than the average

OTHER ARTICLES TO READ
Allergists
HIV/AIDS Counselors and Case Managers
Microbiologists
Oncologists
Physicians
Toxicologists

An epidemiologist works in a maximum containment lab.

Education and Training

High school classes in biology, health, English, physics, and math (including statistics) are recommended. Social studies and geography also are relevant.

A four-year bachelor of science degree is the minimum requirement to enter an epidemiology program in graduate school. Many graduate programs are designed for people who already have a medical degree. Cornell University, for example, requires an M.D. or an R.N. degree plus three years of work experience for entrance into its epidemiology program.

Not every graduate school focuses on the same thing. Johns Hopkins University has programs of study in chronic disease epidemiology, clinical epidemiology, genetics, infectious diseases, and occupational and environmental epidemiology. Case Western Reserve offers a program in genetic epidemiology, while Emory University offers a program in quantitative epidemiology.

Outlook

Job prospects for epidemiologists are promising because there will always be a need to understand, control, and prevent the spread of disease. There is particular promise in the growing field of environmental epidemiology.

Developments in technology, such as genetic recombination and imaging, are changing the field of epidemiology. The use of new information systems will make global communication more comprehensive and efficient between nations.

For More Information

Join science clubs and enter science fairs with projects that focus on biology and chemistry. Volunteer at a health facility to get exposure to medical procedures.

Association for Professionals in Infection Control and Epidemiology
1275 K Street, NW, Suite 1000
Washington, DC 20005-4006
202-789-1890
http://www.apic.org

Centers for Disease Control and Prevention
1600 Clifton Road, NE
Atlanta, GA 30333
800-311-3435
http://www.cdc.gov

Epidemic Intelligence Service Centers for Disease Control and Prevention
1600 Clifton Road, NE
Atlanta, GA 30333
888-496-8347
http://www.cdc.gov/eis

Infectious Diseases Society of America
66 Canal Center Plaza, Suite 600
Alexandria, VA 22314
703-299-0200
http://www.idsociety.org

Ergonomists

SKILLS SPOTLIGHT

◆

What they do
Communicate ideas
Evaluate and manage information
Help clients and customers

Skills they need
Mathematics
Problem solving
Reasoning

What Ergonomists Do

Ergonomists study the workplace to find out how the work environment affects the activities of employees. They research how noise, temperature, and lighting affect workers. They study machines and equipment to make sure they are safe, efficient, and comfortable for the user. Ergonomists educate workers to decrease the number of work-related illnesses and injuries. They also help employers to achieve higher levels of productivity.

According to ergonomic principles, workers should be able to complete a task in several different and safe manners; they should be using the largest appropriate muscle groups; and their joints should be at approximately the middle of their range of movement.

Some ergonomists work on designing new machines and equipment. They do physiological research on how certain types of work-related injuries, such as carpal tunnel syndrome, occur. They study mathematics and physics, in conjunction with the human form, in order to gain a better understanding of how people can avoid performing unsafe and repetitive motions that lead to injury.

Other ergonomists study workplaces and analyze the needs of particular employees in specific work situations. Their clients may be as varied as secretaries, factory workers, and travel agents who suffer from specific physical problems associated with their workplaces. These ergonomists may study assembly-line procedures and suggest changes to reduce monotony and make it easier for workers to load or unload materials. They may also investigate lighting and room temperature, which might influence workers' behavior and productivity. In an office setting, an ergonomist is likely to make suggestions about keyboard placement and monitor height to help avoid injuries. Rearrangement of furniture is often one of the easiest ways to make a workplace safer and more comfortable.

After analyzing data and observing workers, ergonomists submit a written report of their findings and make recommendations

SCHOOL SUBJECTS
Health, Mathematics, Physical education

MINIMUM EDUCATION LEVEL
Master's degree

SALARY RANGE
$31,000 to $52,000 to $80,000

OUTLOOK
About as fast as the average

OTHER ARTICLES TO READ
Chiropractors
Industrial Designers
Industrial Safety and Health Technicians
Interior Designers and Decorators
Kinesiologists
Physical Therapists

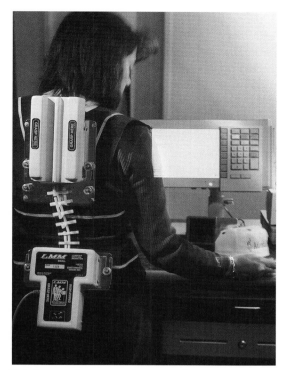

This human factors engineer studies the ergonomics of human performance in simulated zero gravity.

to company representatives for changes in the workplace designed to improve the health, safety, comfort, and productivity of a company's employees.

Education and Training

To be an ergonomist, you need a strong background in mathematics, physical sciences, English, psychology, and statistics. Courses in the life and physical sciences—biology, anatomy, health, and physics—are also helpful, as are classes in research methods, writing, speech, mathematics, and computer science.

Most ergonomists have a bachelor of science degree in a behavioral science (such as psychology or sociology), social science, computer science, or industrial engineering. Course work includes classes in statistics, computer applications, and the health sciences as well as research techniques. The majority of ergonomists also have a master's degree, which is required for most jobs in this field. A doctoral degree is helpful for those who want to teach or work at high levels of management.

Outlook

The employment outlook for ergonomists is good. The public has a better understanding of and appreciation for ergonomy today, and as numerous work environments have become more complex because of technology advances, ergonomists have found a steady demand for their services. Businesses will continue to use ergonomy to reduce worker injury, raise levels of production, and increase profits.

For More Information

Observe your activities and the toll they take on specific parts of your body. Think of the causes of physical problems and different ways you can change your behavior and movements to prevent them.

Board of Certification in Professional Ergonomics
PO Box 2811
Bellingham, WA 98227-2811
888-856-4685
bcpehq@bcpe.org
http://www.bcpe.org

Human Factors and Ergonomics Society
PO Box 1369
Santa Monica, CA 90406
310-394-1811
info@hfes.org
http://www.hfes.org

Event Planners

What Event Planners Do

Event planners oversee all the arrangements that are necessary for meetings and special events. They may be called *meeting, corporate,* or *convention planners,* or *conference coordinators.* They may also be referred to as *meeting managers* or *special event coordinators.*

Event planners have a variety of duties that differ depending on the firms they work for and the events that are being planned. Some event planners are responsible for small in-house meetings, and others are in charge of large conventions or trade shows that are taking place in another area of the country or the world. If a meeting is held in-house, the planner may have to reserve the meeting room; notify attendees of the time, date, and place of the meeting; arrange for refreshments; establish a room layout; print agendas or programs; and arrange for audio-visual equipment.

Planners who organize meetings or events at outside facilities negotiate and contract for meeting rooms, hotel accommodations, air and ground transportation, and food and refreshments. They may also have to schedule speakers, discussion panels, or workshop leaders; publicize the event; hire outside staff; and organize registration procedures.

Planners involved with conventions and trade shows arrange for the transportation of the display booth to the convention site, oversee its setup, arrange for the transportation and lodging of key people attending the event, and assist with the marketing and registration. They also might reserve meeting rooms and a block of guest rooms at a number of nearby hotels for trade show participants and attendees. Managers and planners need to be aware of legal aspects of trade show set-ups such as fire code regulations, floor plans, and space limitations and make sure they are within these guidelines.

Some event planners cater to individuals, groups, or associations and help plan events such as open houses, reunions, anniversaries, and other special occasions. *Party planners* are either self-employed or employed by individuals, families, or small companies to help plan parties for special

SCHOOL SUBJECTS
Business, English, Foreign language

MINIMUM EDUCATION LEVEL
Bachelor's degree

SALARY RANGE
$25,000 to $39,000 to $56,000

OUTLOOK
Faster than the average

OTHER ARTICLES TO READ
Business Managers
Customer Service Representatives
Hotel and Motel Managers and Workers
Travel Agents

occasions. Party planners may help plan celebrations for weddings, birthdays, christenings, bar or bat mitzvahs, anniversaries, retirements, or other events.

Event planners often work erratic hours and long days prior to the event. Travel is often required and the job may include working or traveling nights and on the weekends.

Education and Training

If you are interested in a career as an event planner, take courses in business, English, foreign languages, and speech. Most event planners must have a high school diploma and at least a bachelor's degree. Some colleges offer degrees in meeting planning, but degrees in English, communications, marketing, public relations, sales, or travel would also be a good fit for a career as an event planner.

Outlook

Job opportunities for event planners are expected to grow faster than the average rate for all occupations through 2012. The introduction of new technology enables more meetings to take place than ever before. The majority of planners are women.

For More Information

Searching the Internet for companies that provide event-planning services can give you an idea of the types of services that they offer.

Organize and plan a large family event, such as a birthday, anniversary, graduation, or retirement celebration. You will have to find a location, hire catering or assign family members to bring specific food items,

An event planner discusses the use of conference facilities with the hotel manager.

send invitations, purchase and arrange decorations, and organize entertainment, all according to what your budget allows.

International Association for Exposition Management
8111 LBJ Freeway, Suite 750
Dallas, TX 75251-1313
972-458-8002
http://www.iaem.org

Meeting Professionals International
3030 LBJ Freeway, Suite 1700
Dallas, TX 75234-2759
972-702-3000
http://www.mpiweb.org

Professional Convention Management Association
2301 South Lake Shore Drive, Suite 1001
Chicago, IL 60616-1419
312-423-7262
http://www.pcma.org

Executive Recruiters

What Executive Recruiters Do

Executive recruiters are hired by businesses to place qualified workers in hard-to-fill employment positions. Though many larger companies have in-house human resource departments, they often turn to executive recruiters to handle the responsibilities of locating, researching, and interviewing the best candidates for the job.

There are two kinds of executive search firms: retained or contingent. *Retained recruiters* work with upper-level management positions. They are contracted by a company to fill a particular executive position. Retained recruiters are paid on a flat fee basis, or for a percentage of the candidate's first year's salary and bonus.

Contingency recruiters fill junior- to mid-level executive positions that pay less than $75,000. Many times, companies will notify several firms to fill one position. Contingency recruiters are paid only if their candidate is hired for the job, usually a percentage of the candidate's first year's salary package.

The job of recruiters, whether retained or contingent, begins once the search firm is notified of the job opening and is asked to find the best possible candidate. The recruiter first evaluates the needs and structure of the client or the company. A draft of the job description is made, detailing the title, job description, responsibilities, and salary and benefits package. Once the client approves a written contract, the search begins. Recruiters research candidates by networking with their contacts in the industry. Recruiters also keep informed of industry developments by reading trade papers and magazines as well as national newspapers. Recruiters also receive resumes from people looking to change employment, which they keep on file for future reference.

Recruiters then contact prospective candidates, usually by telephone. Candidates who are interested and qualified are screened further, and references are checked fully. Recruiters conduct personal interviews with the most promising candidates.

SCHOOL SUBJECTS
Business, Psychology

MINIMUM EDUCATION LEVEL
Bachelor's degree

SALARY RANGE
$26,000 to $41,000 to $79,000

OUTLOOK
Faster than the average

OTHER ARTICLES TO READ
Career Counselors
Customer Service Representatives
Labor Union Business Agents
Management Analysts and Consultants
Personnel Specialists

A search for the perfect executive is a lengthy process. Most searches take anywhere from one month to a year or more. Once the position is filled, recruiters conduct one or more follow-ups to make sure the employee's transition into the company is smooth.

Education and Training

Recruiters come from a variety of educational backgrounds, including communications, marketing, and business administration. Many recruiters move into the industry after successful careers in business, health care, banking, or publishing.

A common starting point for recruiters is a position with a contingency firm. Responsibilities may be limited at first, but a successful and consistent work experience could lead to bigger accounts, more placements, higher commissions, a staff position with a retainer search firm, or starting a company of your own.

Outlook

There is a bright future for executive search firms. Potential clients include large international corporations, universities, the government, and smaller businesses. Smaller operations are aware that having a solid executive or administrator may make the difference between turning a profit and not being in business at all.

For More Information

Working part time or as a volunteer in a library can help you learn research skills that are important in recruiting work. Become

An executive recruiter talks with a prospective client.

familiar with business publications, such as the *Wall Street Journal,* the *New York Times, Business Week, Fortune,* and others available at your library. Your guidance counselor can advise you on ways to research careers and qualifications.

The Association of Executive Search Consultants
12 East 41st Street 17th Floor
New York, NY 10017
212-398-9556
aesc@aesc.org
http://www.aesc.org

Kennedy Information
One Phoenix Mill Lane, 5th Floor
Peterborough, NH 03458
800-531-0007
bookstore@kennedyinfo.com
http://www.kennedyinfo.com

National Association of Executive Recruiters
1901 N. Roselle Road, Suite 800
Schaumburg, IL 60195
847-598-3690
http://www.naer.org

Exhibit Designers

What Exhibit Designers Do

Exhibit designers plan, develop, and produce displays for exhibitions at museums and cultural institutions. Designers work with museum educators, curators, and conservators to create educational exhibits that focus on portions of the museum's collection while maintaining safe environmental conditions for the objects on display. Exhibit designers prepare both temporary and permanent exhibitions for a broad range of museum audiences.

Exhibit designers play a key role in helping museums and similar institutions achieve their educational goals. Museums are responsible for providing public access and information about their collections to visitors and scholars. They accomplish their mission by presenting exhibits that display objects and present related information. Because museum visits are interactive experiences, exhibit designers must provide the visiting public with interesting exhibitions that contain visual, auditory, emotional, and intellectual components.

After a decision has been made to construct a new exhibit and a budget has been set, exhibit designers meet regularly with a team of curators, educators, and conservators throughout the exhibit planning stages. They consider the objects to be displayed; the context in which they should be displayed; signage and labeling; explanatory text, charts, graphs, photographs, and maps; lighting; auditory components; interactive components; and visitor traffic patterns. For some objects, exhibit designers need to consider lighting and temperature controls so the items are not damaged while being displayed.

Planning, designing, and producing a new exhibit is costly as well as challenging. Exhibit designers must work creatively during the planning and design stages while remaining flexible in their ideas. During exhibit installation, designers work closely with the production team, which consists of other artists, designers, technicians, computer experts, electricians, and carpenters.

Exhibit designers have additional responsibilities that include extensive research on exhibit topics and investigating new exhibit styles and materials. Some designers also attend conventions of professional associations to network with other designers and share ideas about new approaches to exhibit design and innovative display techniques.

Education and Training

If you are interested in a career as an exhibition designer, you will need a broad educational background. Take courses in English, history, the sciences, art, and foreign language. Because exhibit plans must be drawn to scale and the measurements must be precise, math courses are essential. Math skills are also necessary for developing good budgeting skills. Computer skills are also important, as many designers use computer-aided drafting when planning exhibits. Computer technology is also used in exhibits in order to present information or make them interactive.

Most museums expect exhibit designers to hold a bachelor's degree. Those who

An exhibit designer directs the installation of an architecture show at the Art Institute of Chicago.

desire a position as a director or manager in a museum's design department should consider earning an advanced degree. A degree in museology along with experience in carpentry, building, sculpture, or set design is the best preparation. Some exhibit designers hold degrees in fine art, archaeology, anthropology, or liberal arts.

Outlook

The employment rate of all designers will grow about as fast as the average through 2012, but there is strong competition for museum jobs, which will go to those with many years of experience. Most museums are challenged with budget difficulties, and many choose to contract with independent exhibition and design companies when there is the need to install a new exhibit instead of retaining a staff of in-house designers.

For More Information

Visit museums and cultural centers in your area and observe the design of the exhibits. Designing stage sets for the school drama club or local theater company is good experience.

American Association of Museums
1575 Eye Street, NW, Suite 400
Washington, DC 20005
202-289-1818
http://www.aam-us.org

New England Museum Association
22 Mill Street, Suite 409
Arlington, MA 02476
781 641-0013
http://www.nemanet.org

Export-Import Specialists

What Export–Import Specialists Do

Export-import specialists handle the business arrangements for exporting and importing goods to and from foreign countries. They work out trade agreements with foreign traders and supervise the delivery of the goods. Export-import specialists work for both the government and private industry. There are many kinds of export-import specialists. All specialists must understand international law and be aware of export-import regulations, such as duty fees, but specific responsibilities vary according to the specialty.

Export managers direct foreign sales activities, including negotiating sales and distribution contracts and arranging payment for exported goods. They handle details involved in transporting goods, including licensing agreements, customs declarations, and packing and shipping. They supervise clerical staff in preparing foreign correspondence and other foreign language material, such as sales literature and bid requests.

Customs brokers are intermediaries between importers and the customs service. They prepare entry papers for goods arriving from abroad. They file appropriate documents to allow delivery of foreign goods and to assess import duties and taxes. Customs brokers counsel importers on U.S. rules and regulations, work out any last-minute problems, and arrange for storage of goods in warehouses, if necessary.

Import-export agents are independent contractors who usually work for several clients. They manage activities of import-export firms and coordinate settlements between foreign and domestic buyers and sellers. They plan delivery of goods and supervise workers in the shipping and receiving departments. Agents oversee the assessment of import and export taxes and the granting of entry permits.

Freight forwarders are agents for exporters in moving cargo to overseas destinations.

SCHOOL SUBJECTS
Business, Foreign language, Mathematics

MINIMUM EDUCATION LEVEL
High school diploma

SALARY RANGE
$29,000 to $53,000 to $91,000

OUTLOOK
Faster than the average

OTHER ARTICLES TO READ
Antique and Art Dealers
Business Managers
Buyers
Customs Officials
Economists
Marketing Researchers
Purchasing Agents
Sales Representatives

An export-import specialist discusses the receipt of these boxes with his client by telephone.

and business are helpful. A master's degree in business administration with a specialty in international trade can lead to better job opportunities. Knowing one or more foreign languages is also an advantage.

Export-import specialists find entry-level jobs with the U.S. Customs Service, seaports and airports, and private companies.

Outlook

Opportunities in the export-import field should grow faster than the average rate through the next 10 years. Employment stability in this field is largely dependent on general economic conditions, and job prospects will vary from industry to industry and firm to firm. For example, it may be harder to find work as a textile wholesaler representing a U.S. firm than as a computer wholesaler.

For More Information

Part-time or summer employment in a retail establishment is helpful training for a merchandising career. Read business publications and trade papers to learn all you can about the U.S. trade balance, trade policies, and export and import levels of major goods, such as automobiles.

American Association of Exporters and Importers
1050 17th Street, NW, Suite 810
Washington, DC 20036
202-857-8009
hq@aaei.org
http://www.aaei.org

International Trade Administration
U.S. Department of Commerce
1401 Constitution Avenue, NW
Washington, DC 20230
http://www.ita.doc.gov

They are familiar with the import rules and regulations of foreign countries, methods of shipping, U.S. government export regulations, special packaging or handling restrictions, hazardous materials rules, and the documents connected with foreign trade. Freight forwarders advise clients on freight costs, port charges, consular fees, cost of special documentation, and insurance costs. Forwarders find the most appropriate services so that products are moved by the most timely and cost-effective methods.

Education and Training

Most export-import specialists are college graduates, although a degree is not a requirement. The most useful degrees are in business management, political science, economics, or foreign language. College courses in international trade, marketing,

Family and Consumer Scientists

SKILLS SPOTLIGHT

◆

What they do
Communicate ideas
Help clients and customers
Teach

Skills they need
Problem solving
Reasoning
Speaking/listening

What Family and Consumer Scientists Do

Family and consumer scientists are concerned with the well-being of the home and family. They work in education, dietetics, research, social welfare, extension services, and business. Whatever the job, family and consumer scientists rely on their understanding of food and nutrition, child development, household management, and the many other elements involved in day-to-day living.

Family and consumer scientists who work as teachers in junior and senior high schools teach courses such as nutrition, clothing, child development, family relations, and home management. Teachers at the college level prepare students for careers in home economics. They also conduct research and write articles and textbooks.

Extension-service family and consumer scientists are part of an educational system supported by government agencies to educate and advise families, both rural and urban, on family life, nutrition, child care, and other aspects of homemaking. These scientists offer help and advice over the phone and may travel to various communities to give presentations and assistance.

Health and welfare agencies hire family and consumer scientists to work with social workers, nurses, and physicians. They consult with low-income families who need help with financial management concerns. They develop community programs in health and nutrition, money management, and child care.

The business world offers many opportunities to family and consumer scientists. Some work for manufacturers, where they test and improve products and recipes and prepare booklets on uses of products. They plan educational programs and materials.

Family and consumer scientists who work in media and advertising agencies write about food, fashion, home decor, budgets, and home management. Those

SCHOOL SUBJECTS
Business, Family and consumer science

MINIMUM EDUCATION LEVEL
Bachelor's degree

SALARY RANGE
$23,000 to $38,000 to $67,000

OUTLOOK
Faster than the average

OTHER ARTICLES TO READ
Child Care Workers
Child Life Specialists
Dietitians and Nutritionists
Food Technologists
Home Health Care Aides
Interior Designers and Decorators
Nannies

This consumer and family scientist teacher checks on a rack of iced cinnamon buns that are baking in the classroom's oven.

Many colleges and universities offer these degrees, as well as specialization in subjects such as education, child development, foods and nutrition, dietetics, institution management, textiles and clothing, family economics and home management, household equipment and furnishings, and applied art. Those who conduct research and teach college usually need a master's degree or a doctorate.

Outlook

The demand for family and consumer scientists will be highest for specialists in marketing, merchandising, family and consumer resource management, food service and institutional management, food science and human nutrition, environment and shelter, and textiles and clothing.

who work for retail stores help customers choose furniture and other household items and work in advertising, buying, and merchandising.

Some family and consumer scientists specialize in dietetics. They work in hospitals, hotels, restaurants, or schools. They plan meals, order food and supervise its preparation, handle budgets, and plan special diets.

Family and consumer scientists who work as researchers create products and develop procedures that make life better for families. Researchers work for colleges and universities, government and private agencies, and private companies.

For More Information

Your community 4-H club may offer opportunities in community service, arts, consumer and family sciences, environmental education, and healthy lifestyle education.

American Association of Family and Consumer Sciences
400 N. Columbus Street, Suite 202
703-706-4600
info@aafcs.org
http://www.aafcs.org

National 4-H Council
7100 Connecticut Avenue
Chevy Chase, MD 20815
http://www.fourhcouncil.edu

National Association of Social Workers
750 First Street, NE, Suite 700
Washington, DC 20002-4241
202-408-8600
info@naswdc.org
http://www.naswdc.org

Education and Training

Family and consumer scientists must have at least a bachelor's degree in family and consumer science or home economics.

Farmers

What Farmers Do

Farmers grow crops such as peanuts, corn, wheat, cotton, fruits, or vegetables. They also raise pigs, sheep, poultry, cows, and other animals for meat, dairy products, and other animal products.

Today family farms are disappearing. They are being replaced by large farms run by agricultural corporations that employ farm operators and managers to direct all of the activities on farms. Farm operators may own or rent the land. Farm managers are hired to oversee different farms' operations. The owner of a large crop farm may hire a manager to oversee general planning, another manager to handle planting and harvesting, and a third manager to handle marketing or storing the crops.

There are many different types of farmers. *Diversified crops farmers* grow different combinations of fruits, grains, and vegetables. *General farmers* raise livestock as well as crops. *Cash grain farmers* grow barley, corn, rice, soybeans, and wheat. Other types of farmers include *vegetable farmers; tree-fruit-and-nut crops farmers; field crops farmers,* who raise alfalfa, cotton, hops, peanuts, mint, sugarcane, and tobacco; *animal breeders; fur farmers; livestock ranchers; dairy farmers; poultry farmers; beekeepers; reptile farmers; fish farmers;* and even *worm growers.*

Farmers need good soil and a lot of water for their crops and animals. They need to know how to bring water to their plants (irrigation) and add rich nutrients to the soil (fertilizer). They also need to know how to keep their animals and crops healthy. This involves controlling insects, diseases, and pollution that will damage or destroy crops or livestock. It also involves providing proper care such as clean, warm shelters, proper food, and special breeding programs.

Crop farmers use large farm equipment to turn the soil, plant seeds, gather crops, and store them. Dairy farmers maintain equipment for milking and processing and storing dairy products. As a result, farmers need to know how to run and repair many types of machines. Besides working with the

SCHOOL SUBJECTS
Agriculture, Business

MINIMUM EDUCATION LEVEL
High school diploma

SALARY RANGE
$24,000 to $44,000 to $81,000

OUTLOOK
Decline

OTHER ARTICLES TO READ
Agribusiness Technicians
Agricultural Engineers
Agricultural Scientists
Animal Builders and Technicians
Aquaculturists
Beekeepers
Fishers

An organic farmer windrows wheat on his farm.

soil, crops, animals, and farm machinery, farmers also have to keep extensive records of their income, expenses, and production schedules. They are knowledgeable about the markets for their products and are skilled at negotiating, buying, and selling.

Education and Training

Future farmers can benefit from courses in mathematics and science, especially biology, chemistry, earth science, and botany. Accounting, bookkeeping, business, and computer courses are also very helpful.

There are no specific educational requirements for farmers, but every successful farmer must have knowledge of the principles of soil preparation and cultivation, disease control, and machinery maintenance as well as a mastery of business practices and bookkeeping.

State land-grant universities offer agricultural programs that award bachelor's degrees as well as shorter programs in specific areas. Some universities offer advanced studies in horticulture, animal science, agronomy, and agricultural economics. Most students in agricultural colleges also take courses in farm management, business, finance, and economics. Two-year colleges often have

programs leading to associate's degrees in agriculture.

Outlook

Employment of farmers and ranchers is expected to decline through 2012. Every year can be different for farmers, as production, expansion, and markets are affected by weather, exports, and other factors.

Large corporate farms are fast replacing small farms. Some small-scale farmers, however, have found opportunities in organic food production, farmers' markets, and similar market niches that require direct personal contact with their customers.

Despite the great difficulty in becoming a farmer today, many agriculture-related careers involve people with farm production, marketing, management, and agribusiness.

For More Information

Organizations such as the National FFA Organization (http://www.ffa.org) and 4-H (http://www.fourhcouncil.edu) offer good opportunities for learning about, visiting, and participating in farming activities.

American Farm Bureau Federation
600 Maryland Ave. SW, Suite 800
Washington, DC 20024
202 406-3600
http://www.fb.org

National Council of Farmer Cooperatives
50 F Street, NW, Suite 900
Washington, DC 20001
http://www.ncfc.org

U.S. Department of Agriculture
Washington, DC 20250
202-720-2791
http://www.usda.gov

Fashion Coordinators

What Fashion Coordinators Do

Fashion coordinators produce fashion shows and plan other ways to promote clothing companies and designers. They are employed by design firms, retail corporations, and apparel centers, and some work in the entertainment industry.

Fashion coordinators employed by retail stores, design firms, or shopping centers may produce a monthly fashion show or as many as 50 shows a year. There are different types of fashion shows. Vendor or designer shows arrive at the coordinator's office almost pre-packaged. The outfits are already accessorized and are boxed in the order the clothes should be shown. Commentary and backdrops also are supplied by the vendor or designer. To prepare for a vendor show, fashion coordinators only have to book models and set up a stage. Vendor shows typically take only a few days to produce.

Trend shows are owned by the retailer and are produced by the fashion coordina-tor and his or her staff. Coordinators put outfits and accessories together, choose the choreography and staging, and most importantly, decide on the theme or featured fashion trend. Trend shows are usually produced two or three times a year, and they take a few weeks or a month to produce.

There are several steps to producing a show. First, a budget for the show is set. Then models are selected. Coordinators often use *modeling agents* to find the best men, women, or children. *Stylists* are hired to give the models and their clothes a finished look. *Hairdressers, makeup artists,* and *dressers* prepare the models before the show and during outfit changes. *Production workers* find the right music and lighting. The fashion coordinator and assistants also are responsible for the promotion and execution of a fashion show.

Fashion coordinators promote their store's fashion lines through promotional agreements with on-air television personalities and lending the appropriate clothing to

SCHOOL SUBJECTS
Business, English

MINIMUM EDUCATION LEVEL
Bachelor's degree

SALARY RANGE
$33,000 to $64,000 to $142,000

OUTLOOK
Faster than the average

OTHER ARTICLES TO READ
Cosmetologists
Costume Designers
Event Planners
Fashion Designers
Jewelers
Makeup Artists
Models

television stations, newspapers, and fashion magazines for special fashion shoots.

Education and Training

High school classes that will prepare you for this career include family and consumer science, art, art history, illustration, photography, and business. Some schools, such as the Fashion High School in New York City, offer fashion-related courses such as fashion design, illustration, fashion merchandising, and art and art history along with the more traditional academic classes.

A college education is not required for every fashion job, but a bachelor's degree in fashion design and merchandising, marketing, or other business-related courses will give you an edge. Computer skills are also important.

An internship in the fashion industry is recommended, preferably with a company you hope to work for after graduation

Outlook

Employment in this career should be good for the next decade. Most jobs in the United States will be available in densely populated areas, especially New York City, Chicago, Los Angeles, and Miami.

As fashion trends change, so will the way runway shows are presented. Themes reflect the taste of the fashion consumer—flashy styles translate to loud, heavily choreographed shows; understated clothing may call for softer presentations. One style of show has no spoken commentary. Instead, messages in words and images are shown on the backdrop. More recently, Victoria's Secret produced a show on the Internet. These new and varied types of shows should provide

A fashion coordinator reviews fashion images as she talks with a client on the telephone.

employment opportunities for the creative fashion coordinator.

For More Information

Volunteering at local fashion shows, whether helping models with outfit changes, setting up chairs, or passing out brochures, will give you valuable experience. Produce a fashion show in your high school, using fellow classmates as models and clothing and accessories borrowed from the local mall.

Fashion Group International, Inc.
597 Fifth Avenue, 8th Floor
New York, NY 10017
212-593-1715
http://www.fgi.org

Fashion Institute of Technology
Seventh Avenue at 27th Street
New York, NY 10001-5992
212-217-7999
fitinfo@fitnyc.edu
http://www.fitnyc.edu

National Association of Schools of Art and Design
11250 Roger Bacon Drive, Suite 21
Reston, VA 20190
703-437-0700
info@arts-accredit.org
http://nasad.arts-accredit.org/

Fashion Designers

SKILLS SPOTLIGHT
◆

What they do
Evaluate and manage information
Communicate ideas
Work with a team

Skills they need
Creative thinking
Decision making
Self-esteem

What Fashion Designers Do

Fashion designers design coats, dresses, suits, and other clothing. They may design both outer and inner garments or hats, purses, shoes, gloves, costume jewelry, scarves, or beachwear, or they may specialize in certain types of clothing such as bridal gowns or sportswear. There are only a few top haute-couture designers who produce one-of-a-kind designs for high-fashion houses. Nevertheless, there are thousands of designers who work in the American garment industry creating fashions for mass production and sale to millions of Americans. They work for textile, apparel, and pattern manufacturers; fashion salons; high-fashion department stores, and specialty shops. Some design costumes in the theater and film industries.

In developing a new design or altering an existing one, designers first determine the customers' needs. After a sketch has been prepared, the designer shapes the pattern pieces that make the garment. The pieces are drawn to actual size on paper and then cut out of a fabric, usually muslin. The fabric pieces are sewn together and fitted on a model. The designer modifies pattern pieces, and then a sample garment is made of chosen fabrics. This sample is shown to buyers, and orders are taken for quantities of a single garment or for a full line of clothing in a variety of sizes and colors.

In some companies, designers are involved in all aspects of the production of the line, from the original idea to completed garments. Other designers supervise workrooms, while some work right along with workroom supervisors to solve problems.

Fashion designers often create 50 to 150 designs for each season's showings. They work on spring and summer designs during the fall and winter months and on fall and winter clothing during summer months.

Designers spend time visiting textile manufacturing and sales establishments to learn of the latest fabrics and their uses and

SCHOOL SUBJECTS
Art, Family and consumer science

MINIMUM EDUCATION LEVEL
Some postsecondary training

SALARY RANGE
$28,000 to $55,000 to $113,000

OUTLOOK
About as fast as the average

OTHER ARTICLES TO READ
Costume Designers
Fashion Coordinators
Fashion Editors and Writers
Fashion Illustrators and Photographers
Fashion Models' Agents
Tailors and Dressmakers

capabilities. They browse through stores to see what fashion items are most popular. They meet with marketing and production workers, salespeople, and clients to discover what people are wearing and to discuss ideas and styles.

Education and Training

If you are interested in fashion design, take courses in art, sewing, and computer-aided design (CAD). CAD is increasingly being used by designers to draw designs, make patterns, create prototypes, and reduce design production time and cost.

The best way to become a fashion designer is to complete a two- or three-year program in design from a fashion school. Some colleges offer a four-year degree in fine arts with a major in fashion design. Employers look for designers who have studied mathematics, business, design, sketching, art history, costume history, literature, pattern making, clothing construction, and textiles.

Outlook

Designers make up less than 1 percent of the total number of garment industry workers. Good designers will always be needed, although not in great numbers. Even so, employment of designers is expected to grow about as fast as the average through 2012.

For More Information

Learn to sew well enough to create your own clothing designs. Offer to sew clothing for friends and family members. Visit

A fashion designer fits a dress on a customer in a clothing design studio.

fabric stores to learn about fabrics, trims, patterns, and accessories. Attend fashion shows, visit art galleries, and read fashion magazines, such as *Women's Wear Daily* (http://www.wwd.com).

Custom Tailors and Designers Association of America
The Talley Management Group Inc.
19 Mantua Road
Mt. Royal, NJ 08061
856-423-1621
http://www.ctda.com

Fashion Institute of Technology
Admissions Office
Seventh Avenue at 27th Street
New York, NY 10001-5992
212-217-7999
fitinfo@fitnyc.edu
http://www.fitnyc.edu/

National Association of Schools of Art and Design
11250 Roger Bacon Drive, Suite 21
Reston, VA 20190
703-437-0700
info@arts-accredit.org
http://nasad.arts-accredit.org

Fashion Illustrators and Photographers

SKILLS SPOTLIGHT

◆

What they do
Communicate ideas
Help clients and customers
Select and apply tools/technology

Skills they need
Creative thinking
Problem solving
Self-management

What Fashion Illustrators and Photographers Do

Fashion illustrators and photographers work in a glamorized, intense environment. The focus of their art is styles of clothing. They work for advertising agencies, the news media, catalog houses, and fashion magazines.

Photographers' tools include cameras, film, filters, lenses, tripods, and lighting equipment. Those who develop their own film have darkroom facilities. Fashion photographers sometimes choose locations for shoots, such as beaches or train stations, or they may construct studio sets. They work with a team of people, including designers, editors, models, photo stylists, hair stylists, and makeup artists to create shots that make the clothes and the models look good. Catalog shots tend to be straightforward, showing as much detail in the clothing as possible. Photographs for fashion magazines and advertisements are often more creative, conveying a particular mood and lifestyle.

Fashion illustrators also work with creative teams. Their tools are pencils, pastels, charcoals, paints, palettes, papers, drawing boards, as well as computers. Illustrators often become known for a particular medium or a special style. As with photographs, illustrations must be accurate in detail and attractive enough to entice customers to buy the clothing shown.

Fashion photographers and illustrators are often freelancers. They find business by showing their portfolios and working for several clients. Freelancers operate small businesses. They secure clients, and handle accounting, tax payments, and other aspects of running a business. The fashion world is fast-paced and competitive. The hours can be long and the pressure intense to produce good work under tight deadlines. Photographers and illustrators may have to face rejection of their work when they are starting out until they can earn a reputation and develop a style that is in demand.

SCHOOL SUBJECTS
Art, Business

MINIMUM EDUCATION LEVEL
Some postsecondary training

SALARY RANGE
$14,000 to $27,000 to $100,000+

OUTLOOK
About as fast as the average

OTHER ARTICLES TO READ
Artists
Fashion Designers
Graphic Designers
Illustrators
Photo Stylists
Photographers

Education and Training

There are no formal education requirements for fashion illustrators or photographers. Many high schools offer photography classes, and most offer art courses. For both photographers and illustrators, the best education is practice.

As your skills improve, you will begin to build a portfolio of your work, or a collection of your best sketches or photos. Some vocational or fashion schools offer classes in fashion illustration, where you learn art techniques as well as how to assemble and present your portfolio. Photography programs are widely available from the associate's to the bachelor's degree level. Photographers can apprentice with established photographers.

Outlook

Employment for visual artists and photographers is expected to grow as fast as the average through 2012. For photographers and illustrators working specifically in fashion, employment will likely depend on the economic health of magazines, newspapers, advertising firms, fashion houses and other fashion-related businesses. The outlook for these businesses currently looks strong. In addition, the rise of e-zines and retail Web sites will create a need for illustrators and photographers.

For More Information

Take drawing and photography classes offered by your school or a community center. Join a school photography or art club to meet others who share your interests. Join the staff of the school yearbook, newspaper, or literary magazine. Keep up with

A fashion illustrator sketches a dress design.

fashion trends and styles by reading fashion magazines and catalogs.

Fashion Institute of Technology
Seventh Avenue at 27th Street
New York, NY 10001-5992
212-217-7999
http://www.fitnyc.edu

Savannah College of Art and Design
PO Box 2072
Savannah, GA 31402-2072
800-869-7223
info@scad.edu
http://www.scad.edu

Society of Illustrators
128 East 63rd Street
New York, NY 10021-7303
212-838-2560
http://www.societyillustrators.org

Fashion Models' Agents

What Fashion Models' Agents Do

Fashion models' agents act as the link bringing together fashion models and their clients. They match models to jobs according to a particular look the client desires. Agents arrange for promising models to work with professional photographers, stylists, and other fashion consultants in order to enhance the models' appearance and develop their style. Agents promote their models to potential clients.

An agent's job may begin when a client contacts the agency with a possible job assignment. The client, for example, a retail store or an advertising agency, usually will have a specific "look" in mind for the model. The look may include such aspects as the model's hair color, age group, body type, or ethnicity. The agent may then send a group of models to the client for an audition.

Many times an agent is also responsible for arranging a photo shoot for the model as well as transportation if the assignment is out of town. The agency is responsible for billing the client and making certain the model is paid for his or her work. In return, the agency earns a commission from the model, which is typically 15 to 20 percent of the model's total earnings, as well as a commission from the client, which is usually about 20 percent. Due to the short-lived careers of most models, agents now wisely provide them with financial planning and advice.

Agents often help newer models prepare their portfolio, which provides a list of a model's previous assignments and tearsheets (examples of their work "torn out" of magazines or other publications).

While agents maintain good working relationships with established clients, they also look for new clients and more assignment possibilities. Agents attend modeling shows and conventions to scout for young people, interview and access their modeling potential, and sign these promising new talents to modeling contracts.

Education and Training

A high school diploma is necessary for work as a fashion model agent. If you are interested in pursuing this career, you should concentrate on classes such as family and consumer science, art, business, mathematics, English, and speech. Some high schools offer curriculum targeted to fashion, which may include classes in design, illustration, and sewing.

While a college degree is helpful, you do not necessarily need one to get ahead in this industry. Much of the training is learned while on the job. In essence, a model is a commodity you are trying to sell; so naturally, any sales experience you have is good. On-the-job training, including working as an assistant, learning to do bookings, keeping track of schedules, and meeting with clients will be useful. In this business, your contacts are extremely important.

Fashion models' agents work to place their clients on go–sees and to land them appearances or parts in commercials, fashion shows, and print ads.

Job Outlook

Employment in this field should grow faster than the average through 2012. Since most clients prefer to work with modeling agencies, very few models succeed without the support of an agency. New York City will continue to be the hub of modeling in the United States, and many large agencies will stay headquartered there. Some agents also represent parts models—those that model specific body parts. The most popular parts models specialize in modeling legs, feet, or hands.

Competition for jobs will most likely be stiff since many people view the fashion industry as glamorous and high paying. In truth, many careers in this field are short-lived, the result of trends and looks falling out of favor.

For More Information

You can hone your sales and marketing abilities by getting a part-time or seasonal job at any retail store. Attend a model convention or search. You will be able to observe the process potential models go through as well as see agents at work.

Fashion Institute of Technology (FIT)
Seventh Avenue at 27th Street
New York, NY 10001-5992
212-217-7999
fitinfo@fitsnyc.edu
http://www.fitnyc.edu

The Insider's Guide to Supermodels and Modeling
http://www.supermodelguide.com

Models.com
http://models.com

Fashion Writers and Editors

What Fashion Writers and Editors Do

Fashion writers express, promote, and interpret fashion ideas and facts in written form. *Fashion editors* perform a wide range of functions. However, their primary responsibility is to ensure that text provided by fashion writers is suitable in content, format, and style for the intended audiences. Fashion writers and editors are typically employed by newspaper, magazine, and book publishers; *radio and television stations,* and online publications. Some fashion writers and editors are also employed by fashion houses and advertising agencies.

Fashion writers, also known as *fashion reporters, correspondents,* or *authors,* express their ideas about fashion in words for books, magazines, newspapers, advertisements, radio, television, and the Internet. These writing jobs require a combination of creativity and hard work.

Good fashion writers gather as much information as possible about their subject and then carefully check the accuracy of their sources. This can involve extensive library research, interviews, and long hours of observation and personal experience. Generally, their writing will be reviewed, corrected, and revised by their editors and by themselves many times before a final copy is ready for publication.

Fashion editors work with fashion writers on the staffs on newspapers, magazines, publishing houses, radio or television stations, and corporations of all kinds. Their primary responsibility is to make sure that text provided by fashion writers is suitable in content, format, and style for the intended audiences.

Editors must make sure that all text to be printed is well written, factually correct (sometimes this job is done by a *researcher* or *fact checker*), and grammatically correct. Other editors, including *managing editors,*

SCHOOL SUBJECTS
English, Family and consumer science, Journalism

MINIMUM EDUCATION LEVEL
Bachelor's degree

SALARY RANGE
$23,000 to $44,000 to $91,000

OUTLOOK
About as fast as the average

OTHER ARTICLES TO READ
Copy Editors
Copywriters
Fashion Coordinators
Fashion Designers
Fashion Illustrators
Fashion Models' Agents
Magazine Editors
Writers

During Fashion Week, a posh fashion editor critiques an evening gown as the model sashays down the runway.

editors in chief, and *editorial directors,* have managerial responsibilities and work with heads of other departments, such as marketing, sales, and production.

Education and Training

Fashion writers and editors must learn to write well, so it is important to take English, journalism, and communications courses in high school. To gain a better perspective on fashion and design, take classes in family and consumer science, including sewing and design. Since much of the fashion industry is based overseas, taking classes in a foreign language, such as French, will also be beneficial. In addition, computer and word processing courses will help you learn how to type quickly and accurately.

A college education is usually necessary if you want to become a writer or editor. Fashion writers and editors must be knowledgeable about their subject, so classes—or even degrees—in fashion design and marketing are also strongly recommended.

Outlook

Employment opportunities in writing and editing are expected to increase about as fast as the average for all occupations through 2012, according to the U.S. Department of Labor. However, because of the narrow scope of fashion writing and editing, competition for jobs will be very intense.

For More Information

To improve your writing skills, read as much as you can. Fiction, nonfiction, poetry, and essays will introduce you to many different forms of writing. You can also work as a reporter, writer, or editor on school newspapers, yearbooks, and literary magazines.

Fashion Group International Inc.
8 West 40th Street, 7th Floor
New York, NY 10018
212-302-5511
info@fgi.org
http://www.fgi.org

Magazine Publishers of America
810 Seventh Avenue, 24th Floor
New York, NY 10019
mpa@magazine.org
http://www.magazine.org

National Association of Schools of Art and Design
11250 Roger Bacon Drive, Suite 21
Reston, VA 20190-5248
703-437-0700
info@arts-accredit.org
http://nasad.arts-accredit.org

Fast Food Workers

What Fast Food Workers Do

Fast food workers are employed by hamburger joints, coffee shops, hot dog stands, delicatessens, and other places that promise a quick bite to eat. These workers grill meats, prepare french fries, make sandwiches and salads, keep condiment containers filled, and provide hot and cold beverages. They take and fill customers' orders, run the cash register, and keep the restaurant clean. Most fast food restaurants are open seven days a week, and some operate 24 hours a day. To service a fast-moving community, fast food workers are required to keep a restaurant efficient, tidy, and comfortable.

Most fast food restaurants employ people who can do a variety of tasks. They use many different machines and appliances, including fryers, grills, soft-serve ice cream machines, blenders, coffee machines, and soda fountains. They use kitchen tools, such as knives, graters, tongs, and measuring spoons and cups.

Fast food workers who are part of the kitchen staff may begin as assistants to the trained cooks. These assistants may help set up supplies, refill condiment containers, or do prep work such as slicing meats or vegetables. These assistants also may be responsible for general cleanup duties in the kitchen area. Kitchen staff employees who cook are responsible for preparing all food to meet the company's standards.

The *cashier* in a fast food restaurant is responsible for taking the customers' orders, entering orders into the computer or cash register, taking payment, and returning proper change. In some fast food establishments, the cashier may fill the customers' orders and serve them to customers on trays or in carryout containers. It is often the cashier's duty to greet customers, welcoming them to the restaurant in a friendly and courteous way. Since these employees are responsible for interacting with customers, they are required to keep their immediate workstations clean and neat.

Some fast food workers take and deliver orders from the drive-thru using an intercom system. They also handle money and make change. Although they must work

SCHOOL SUBJECTS
Business, Family and consumer science

MINIMUM EDUCATION LEVEL
High school diploma

SALARY RANGE
$11,960 to $15,770 to $26,020+

OUTLOOK
About as fast as the average

OTHER ARTICLES TO READ
Cooks, Chefs, and Bakers
Counter and Retail Clerks
Food Production Workers
Food Service Workers
Restaurant Managers

quickly and may have a long line of customers, fast food workers always need to remain friendly and courteous.

Some fast food chains offer workers the chance to work full time and advance into management positions. As workers gain more experience, they may be given more responsibilities, such as arranging work schedules, supervising and training other employees, opening and closing the restaurant, and interviewing potential employees.

Most fast food workers work part time or temporarily, since fast food restaurants provide good employment opportunities for students, parents of small children, people who are changing jobs or need a second job, the elderly, and people with disabilities.

Education and Training

There are no formal education requirements for fast food workers. When hiring, managers look for applicants with a neat appearance, a courteous and friendly manner, and a desire to work hard. Employees receive training on the job. Skills learned in a fast food environment are easily transferable to jobs in other types of restaurants or retail stores.

Outlook

Americans are eating more frequently at full-service restaurants today, so employment growth is expected to be limited for fast food workers, especially cooks. Also, job growth for fast food cooks is expected to be slower than the average, as their duties are combined with those of other workers. Despite this trend, job opportunities for all types of food and beverage workers are

A drive-thru-window order taker doubles as an order filler during slow times.

expected to be plentiful for the next decade or more. There is extremely high turnover among fast food workers, so most openings will result from a need to replace workers who have moved on. Entry-level jobs are not difficult to find.

For More Information

Develop your cooking skills. Look for opportunities to work in the school cafeteria, or volunteer at a community soup kitchen. Hosting or working at a registration desk for school events will give you experience in customer service.

National Restaurant Association
1200 17th Street, NW
Washington, DC 20036
202-331-5900
http://www.restaurant.org

National Restaurant Association Educational Foundation
175 West Jackson Boulevard, Suite 1500
Chicago, IL 60604-2814
800-765-2122
http://www.nraef.org

FBI Agents

SKILLS SPOTLIGHT
♦
What they do
Communicate ideas
Evaluate and manage information
Exercise leadership

Skills they need
Integrity/honesty
Problem-solving
Speaking/listening

What FBI Agents Do

The Federal Bureau of Investigation (FBI) is a government agency that trains special agents or investigators to report on people who are suspected of crimes against the United States. They track down criminals who have broken federal laws. These crimes include bank robbery, kidnapping, interstate transportation of stolen property, mail fraud, theft, spying against the United States (espionage), and destroying U.S. property (sabotage).

FBI agents usually work alone, unless there is potential danger or the case demands two or more people. Assignments are top secret and often dangerous, and discussed only among other authorized bureau members. Agents may not talk about their work with family or friends.

The bureau and its agents work closely with national and international law enforcement agencies. Agents wear ordinary clothes so they won't bring attention to themselves, but carry some form of identification to prove they are acting on behalf of the U.S. government. Those involved in dangerous work carry guns for protection.

Agents may need to travel for extended periods or live in various cities. Special agents may be assigned to one of 56 field offices, FBI headquarters in Washington D.C., or to resident agencies, which report to field offices. Agents may interview people to gather information, spend time searching various types of records, and observe people, especially those suspected of criminal intentions or acts. FBI agents take part in arrests and may participate in or lead raids of various kinds. Sometimes, they are summoned to testify in court cases regarding their investigations and findings.

Agents send their reports and evidence to the criminal laboratory at FBI headquarters. There they are filed in various departments, such as fingerprinting, firearms, documents, or photography. This information is then readily available to United States law enforcement agencies for use in their cases.

SCHOOL SUBJECTS
Accounting, Foreign language, Government

MINIMUM EDUCATION LEVEL
Bachelor's degree

SALARY RANGE
$39,115 to $61,251 to $90,480+

OUTLOOK
About as fast as the average

OTHER ARTICLES TO READ
Crime Analysts
Deputy U.S. Marshals
Detectives
Police Officers
Secret Service Special Agents
Spies

Education and Training

To become an FBI agent, you must be a citizen of the United States, at least 23 years old, have a valid driver's license, be available for assignment anywhere in the bureau's jurisdiction (including Puerto Rico), and be in excellent physical condition. You must pass a color-vision test, a hearing test, a physical fitness exam, and a background check.

At least one of the following qualifications is necessary: a law-school degree; fluency in a foreign language; or a bachelor's degree with a major in accounting, engineering, or computer science. If your major is not specialized, you need either three years of full-time work experience following college or a graduate degree and two years of work experience. In addition, applicants must pass a series of oral and written examinations that test knowledge of law and accounting and ability to investigate crimes.

New agents undergo an extensive 16-week training program at the FBI Academy at Quantico, Virginia. After training, agents work a one-year probationary period under the supervision of a senior agent. If they are found fit after a year, they are hired permanently.

Searching through old files and new faxes, an FBI agent collects information on suspects in a crime.

recruitment, though, hiring of agents will remain somewhat limited, and competition for openings will continue to be extremely high.

Outlook

As of April 2005, approximately 12,406 special agents worked for the FBI. Most job vacancies will arise as agents retire, advance, or resign. Turnover is low, as most agents remain with the FBI throughout their working lives.

Recent increases in organized crime, white-collar crime, and terrorist threats on American soil have led the FBI to increase the number of agents. Despite increased

For More Information

Ask your librarian to help you find books and other resources on the FBI and crime fighting. Visit the FBI Kids & Youth Educational Page at http://www.fbi.gov/kids/6th12th/6th12th.htm.

Federal Bureau of Investigation
935 Pennsylvania Avenue, NW
Washington, DC 20535
202-324-3000
http://www.fbi.gov

Fiber Optics Technicians

What Fiber Optics Technicians Do

Fiber optics technicians prepare, install, and test fiber optics transmission systems. These systems are composed of fiber optic cables and allow data to be sent between computers, phones, and faxes. Technicians who work for telecommunications companies install lines for local area networks, which serve small areas of linked computers, such as in an office.

A telecommunications company contracts with other companies to create communications systems. A salesman evaluates the customer's need and then orders the materials for the installation. Fiber optics technicians take these materials to the job site. First, they walk through the area where the fiber optic cables are to be installed. They look at detailed plans for the cable installation and the building. They evaluate and discuss procedures with the client. Newer buildings are readily equipped for installation, but in older buildings, it may be more difficult to install cables behind ceiling tiles and in the walls. Technicians may have to climb ladders or work beneath floorboards.

After technicians prepare an area for cable, they run the cable from the computer's main frame to individual workstations. Technicians may have to fuse fibers together. This procedure requires steady hands and good eyesight. They clean the fiber and cut it with a special diamond-headed cleaver. After both ends are prepared, technicians place them into a fusion splicer. At the press of a button, the splicer fuses the two fibers together.

When workstations have been connected, technicians test the cable using power meters and other devices by running a laser through it. The testing equipment measures the amount of time it takes for the laser to pass through and indicates any signal loss or faults in the fiber link.

Some fiber optics technicians work as assemblers, spending most of their time sitting at a bench. Some work out in the field installing or repairing fiber beneath the ground.

SCHOOL SUBJECTS
Mathematics, Technical/shop

MINIMUM EDUCATION LEVEL
High school diploma

SALARY RANGE
$35,646 to $40,767 to $47,404+

OUTLOOK
Faster than the average

OTHER ARTICLES TO READ
Electronics Engineering Technicians
Electronics Service Technicians
Line Installers and Cable Splicers
Telecommunications Technicians
Telephone Installers and Repairers

A fiber optics technician repairs communication lines.

Education and Training

Shop classes will give you experience working with hand and power tools. Math and physics courses are helpful as well.

A college degree isn't required, but it can give you an edge when looking for work as a fiber optics technician. A number of community colleges across the country offer programs in fiber optics technology or broadband networks technology. These programs offer such courses as cable construction, fiber optic installation techniques, single-mode and multimode systems, and wavelength and bandwidth. They also may include lab and certification components. Some schools may also offer short-term training programs.

Certification may be available from local community colleges and training programs, as well as from professional organizations such as The Fiber Optic Association.

Outlook

Digital transmissions will soon be the norm for telecommunications. Not only do modern offices require data communications systems, but cable companies are also investing in fiber optics to offer digital TV and cable as well as quality phone service. Also, the cost of fiber is dropping, which means more companies will invest in fiber optics. As a result, experienced fiber optics assemblers and installers will find plenty of job opportunities in the next decade.

For More Information

There are a great many sources of information about developments in fiber optics and the telecommunications industry, including Fiber Optic Technology (http://www.fpnmag.com). To read about the history of fiber optics, see *City of Light: The Story of Fiber Optics* (Sloan Technology Series) by Jeff Hecht (Oxford University Press, 1999).

The Fiber Optic Association
1110 South Mission Road, #355
Fallbrook, CA 92028
760-452-3655
info@thefoa.org
http://www.thefoa.org

Optical Society of America
2010 Massachusetts Avenue, NW
Washington, DC 20036-1023
202-223-8130
info@osa.org
http://www.osa.org

Film and Television Directors

What Film and Television Directors Do

Most positions in the film industry are free-lance jobs, which means workers are hired for the duration of a project. *Film and television directors* coordinate the production of a film or show and are involved in every stage, from hiring actors to editing the final film.

Producers are in charge of the production's business and financial side, while directors are in charge of the creative and technical aspects. Producers usually hire directors and they work closely together. They review scripts and develop budgets and production schedules, including time for researching, filming, and editing.

Directors give directions to many people, such as costume designers, set designers, art directors, composers, and choreographers. During rehearsals and filming, they plan the action carefully, telling actors how to move and interpret scripts, helping them give their best performances. Directors also monitor the filming crew. They direct sets and lights, and decide on the sequence and angles of camera shots. Filming of a movie or show is completed out of order, so directors have to visualize how everything will fit together at the end. Once filming is finished, directors supervise film editing and the addition of sound and special effects.

Film and television directors work in many different forms, including feature films, television commercials, documentaries, animated films, music videos, and instructional videos. Most directors specialize in one type of film or show.

Some television directors work on regular shows, such as soap operas, sporting events, news programs, talk shows, and game shows. They work at a console with a row of television monitors, which display what's going on in different parts of the studio. Directors then choose which camera shots to broadcast.

SCHOOL SUBJECTS
English, Theater/dance

MINIMUM EDUCATION LEVEL
Bachelor's degree

SALARY RANGE
$23,300 to $46,240 to $119,760+

OUTLOOK
About as fast as the average

OTHER ARTICLES TO READ
Art Directors
Cinematographers
Film and Television Editors
Film and Television Producers
Radio and Television Program Directors
Screenwriters

Education and Training

Studying literature and composition exposes you to diverse storytelling techniques. Theater classes provide the opportunity to work with actors, and photography and film courses teach visual composition.

Movie or television directors do not need specific educational backgrounds, but the most successful ones have a combination of talent and experience as well as good business and management skills.

A great way to begin a career as a director is to build a reputation in the industry, starting at a small television station, community theater or film production studio. Many directors have experience as actors or in some other capacity within the industry.

The Directors Guild of America offers an Assistant Directors Training Program to individuals with an associate's degree or two years of experience in movie or television production. Many colleges and film schools also offer courses in film, stage directing, acting, set design, and production.

Outlook

Employment for motion picture and television directors is expected to grow as fast as the average through 2012. Global demand for films and television programming made in the United States is growing, and demand for home video and DVD rentals is strong. Competition is extreme, however, and turnover is high.

For More Information

Watch films and study them. Many DVDs now include behind-the-scenes footage, including directors' comments, alternate endings, and cut scenes, which will teach you much about the directing process. Read trade publications, such as *Hollywood Reporter* (http://www.hollywoodreporter.com) and *Variety* (http://www.variety.com).

American Film Institute
2021 North Western Avenue
Los Angeles, CA 90027-1657
323-856-7600
http://www.afi.com

Broadcast Education Association
1771 N Street, NW
Washington, DC 20036-2891
888-380-7222
beainfo@beaweb.org
http://www.beaweb.org

Directors Guild of America
7920 Sunset Boulevard
Los Angeles, CA 90046
310-289-2000
http://www.dga.org

A television director directs a production from behind a mixing board in a television production room.

Film and Television Editors

What Film Editors Do

Film and television editors perform an important role in the creation of films, videos, and television commercials. They use special equipment to alter an unedited movie or videotape and arrange the material to create effective films. They work with producers and directors from the earliest phases of filming and production. Producers explain the objectives and larger scope, and directors discuss story lines, scenes, and camera angles, all of which helps editors understand how to approach their work.

Once filming is complete, film and television editors choose the segments to be used. Sometimes scenes have several takes, so editors select segments with the best film or video quality, dramatic value, or other criteria. Editors refer to scripts and director's notes when making their choices. They time the film or video segments to specified lengths and reassemble them in a sequence that makes the most sense and has the greatest impact. Editors and directors review the reassembled material on a video monitor, and editors make further adjustments until all are satisfied.

Editing a feature film or documentary can take six to nine months. Editing music videos and television commercials takes less time.

Film editors are using nonlinear processes more often, in which the film is transferred to a digital format. A computer database tracks individual frames and stores the scenes as information folders on computer hard drives. Editors can quickly access scenes and frames with the click of a mouse.

Sound editors work on film and television soundtracks. They keep libraries of sounds for various projects, including natural sounds such as thunder or raindrops, animal noises, or musical interludes. Some sound editors specialize in music, and others work with sound effects. They may use unusual objects, machines, or computer-generated noisemakers to create desired sounds.

SCHOOL SUBJECTS
Art, English

MINIMUM EDUCATION LEVEL
Some postsecondary training

SALARY RANGE
$20,300 to $38,370 to $78,070+

OUTLOOK
About as fast as the average

OTHER ARTICLES TO READ
Audio Recording Engineers
Broadcast Engineers
Film and Television Directors
Film and Television Producers
Radio and Television Program Directors

Education and Training

Training to be a film or television editor takes many years. The best educational background is in the liberal arts. Some studios require film or television editors to have bachelor's degrees, with majors in English, journalism, theater, or film. Some community and two-year colleges offer film study programs with courses in film and video editing. Universities with broadcast journalism departments also offer film and video editing courses and may have contacts at local television stations. The American Film Institute offers listings of colleges with film courses, and graduate film schools.

An apprenticeship is an excellent way to gain exposure to the business. By working closely with an editor, an apprentice can learn television or film operations and specific film-editing techniques.

Outlook

Employment of film and television editors is expected to grow about as fast as the average through 2012. The growth of cable television and an increase in the number of independent film studios will increase the demand for editors, but competition will remain keen.

The digital revolution greatly affects the editing process. Editors will work much more closely with special effects experts on projects. Digital technology may allow some prospective editors more direct routes into the industry, but the majority of editors will have to follow traditional routes, obtaining years of experience.

This film editor splices a newly shot film.

For More Information

Join a film or video club at your school or community center. Watch different films and television shows. Experiment with one of the many digital film-editing systems available for home computers. Feed your own digital video into your computers, then edit the material and add your own special effects and titles.

American Cinema Editors
100 Universal City Plaza
Building 2352 B, Room 202
Universal City, CA 91608
http://www.ace-filmeditors.org

American Film Institute
2021 North Western Avenue
Los Angeles, CA 90027-1657
http://www.afi.com

The National Television Academy
111 West 57th Street, Suite 600
New York, NY 10019
http://www.emmyonline.org

Film and Television Producers

SKILLS SPOTLIGHT

◆

What they do
Allocate funds and resources
Communicate ideas
Exercise leadership

Skills they need
Decision Making
Problem Solving
Responsibility

What Film and Television Producers Do

Film and television producers organize and secure financial backing for films and television shows. A producer's job begins with the selection of a movie idea from a script or other material. Some films are made from original screenplays, and others are adapted from books. If a book is selected, the producer first purchases the rights from the author or publishing company and hires a writer to transform the book into a screenplay.

After selecting a project, the producer finds a director, technical crew, and lead actors for the film. These essential people, along with the script and screenwriter, are referred to as "the package," and it is this package that the producer tries to sell to an investor to raise the necessary funds to finance the film.

There are three common sources for financing a film: major studios, production companies, and individual investors. Major studios are the largest source of money and finance most of the big-budget films. Producers of documentary films approach individual donors; foundations; art agencies of federal, state, and local governments; and even family members and churches.

Producers can spend a great deal of time raising money from individual investors. They fund raise by telephone as well as in conferences, at business lunches, and even at cocktail parties.

After raising the money, the producer takes the basic plan of the package and tries to work it into a developed project. The script may be rewritten several times, a full cast of actors is hired, salaries are negotiated, and the filming location is chosen.

During the production phase, the producer tries to keep the project on schedule and the spending within the established budget. Other production tasks include reviewing dailies, which are prints of the day's filming. The producer is responsible for resolving all problems, including personal conflicts among employees. If the

SCHOOL SUBJECTS
Business, English

MINIMUM EDUCATION LEVEL
High school diploma

SALARY RANGE
$23,300 to $46,240 to $119,760+

OUTLOOK
About as fast as the average

OTHER ARTICLES TO READ
Cinematographers
Film and Television Directors
Film and Television Editors
Fund-Raisers
Music Producers

film is successfully completed, the producer monitors its distribution and may participate in publicity and advertising.

To accomplish the many varied tasks of the position, producers hire a number of subordinates, such as associate producers, sometimes called co-producers, line producers, and production assistants. Job titles vary from project to project.

Education and Training

English composition and speech courses will help you develop writing and communication skills. Business and economics courses can prepare you for the financial responsibilities of a producer's job.

Many producers have taken formal courses at a college or a university or have attended special film programs. This is helpful, but experience is the best qualification. Most producers work their way into the position from other film-related jobs, such as production, acting, editing, and directing. It is important to have contacts in the industry and with potential investors.

Outlook

Employment for producers is expected to grow as fast as the average through 2012. Opportunities may increase with the expansion of cable and satellite television, news programs, video and DVD rentals, and an increased overseas demand for American-made films, but competition for jobs will be strong. Live theater and entertainment will also provide job openings.

For More Information

Join a film or video club. Experience with theater productions can be useful, especially

A producer works behind the scenes of a television show, monitoring and coordinating program production.

in a fund-raising capacity. Volunteer to work on committees that organize, raise funds for, produce, and publicize special events at your school. Community cable stations may hire volunteers or offer internships.

American Film Institute
2021 North Western Avenue
Los Angeles, CA 90027-1657
323-856-7600
http://www.afi.com

The National Television Academy
111 West 57th Street, Suite 600
New York, NY 10019
212-586-8424
http://www.emmyonline.org

Producers Guild of America Inc.
8530 Wilshire Boulevard, Suite 450
Beverly Hills, CA 90211
310-358-9020
info@producersguild.org
http://www.producersguild.org

Financial Analysts

What Financial Analysts Do

Financial analysts study the financial situations of companies and recommend ways for these companies to manage, spend, and invest their money. They work for banks, brokerage firms, government agencies, mutual funds, and insurance and investment companies.

Financial analysts are sometimes called *investment analysts* or *security analysts*. Their analysis begins with an examination of the company's financial history and objectives, income and expenditures, risk tolerance, and current investments. Once they understand the employer's or client's financial standing and investment goals, financial analysts research other companies that the employer or client may want to invest in. They investigate each company's history, past and potential earnings, and products. Based on their findings, financial analysts may recommend that their employer or client buy stock in these companies.

Financial analysts also research companies that their employer or client already invests in, to determine whether stocks

should be held, sold, or if more stock should be purchased.

Financial analysts compile various reports on their employer or client and on investment opportunities, such as profit-and-loss statements and quarterly outlook statements. They help develop budgets, analyze and oversee cash flow, and perform cost-benefit analyses. They conduct risk analyses to determine what the employer or client can risk at a given time. They also ensure that their employer or client meets tax or regulatory requirements.

Many specialties fall under the job title of financial analyst. *Budget analysts* look at a company's operating costs or its individual departments, and prepare budget reports. *Credit analysts* examine credit records to determine the potential risk in extending credit or lending money. *Investment analysts* evaluate investment data so they can make suitable investment recommendations. *Mergers and acquisitions analysts* conduct research and make recommendations relating to company mergers

---

SCHOOL SUBJECTS
Business, Computer science,
    Mathematics

MINIMUM EDUCATION LEVEL
Bachelor's degree

SALARY RANGE
$34,570 to $57,100 to $108,060

OUTLOOK
About as fast as the average

OTHER ARTICLES TO READ
Accountants
Bank Examiners
Credit Analysts
Financial Planners
Risk Managers

and acquisitions. *Risk analysts* focus on evaluating the risks of investments. *Security analysts* study securities, such as stocks and bonds. *Tax analysts* prepare, file, and examine federal, state, and local tax payments and returns for their employer or client.

Education and Training

Math, accounting, business, and computer classes are important. Most employers require financial analysts to hold a bachelor's degree in accounting, business administration, finance, or statistics. Other possible majors include communications, international business, and public administration.

Financial analysts continue to take courses to keep up with changes in the financial world, including international trade, state and federal laws and regulations, and computer technology.

Financial analysts can earn the Chartered Financial Analyst (CFA) charter from the Association for Investment Management and Research. Many employers expect job seekers to be CFA charterholders. Some firms require that you have a certified public accountant license.

Outlook

Economic conditions and the stock market have a direct effect on the employment outlook for financial analysts. When the economy is doing well, companies are more likely to make investments and will need financial analysts. When the economy is down, companies are less likely to make investments, and there will be less need for financial analysts. International securities markets, the complexity of financial products, and business mergers and acquisitions are expected to maintain the demand for financial analysts.

A financial analyst reviews paperwork on a client's financial standing.

For More Information

Read publications such as *Barron's* (http://www.barrons.com), the *Wall Street Journal* (http://www.wsj.com), *Forbes* (http://www.forbes.com), *Business Week* (http://www.businessweek.com), *Fortune* (http://www.fortune.com), and *Financial Times* (http://www.ft.com). Volunteer to handle the bookkeeping for a school club, or help balance the family checking account to become familiar with simple bookkeeping practices.

Association for Financial Professionals
7315 Wisconsin Avenue, Suite 600 West
Bethesda, MD 20814
http://www.afponline.org

Association for Investment Management and Research
PO Box 3668
560 Ray C. Hunt Drive
Charlottesville, VA 22903-0668
http://www.aimr.org

U.S. Securities and Exchange Commission Office of Investor Education and Assistance
100 F Street, NE
Washington, DC 20549
help@sec.gov
http://www.sec.gov

Financial Planners

SKILLS SPOTLIGHT

♦

What they do
Communicate ideas
Evaluate and manage information
Help clients and customers

Skills they need
Mathematics
Reading/writing
Speaking/listening

What Financial Planners Do

Financial planners advise their clients on many aspects of finance. Although they seem to be knowledgeable about many areas, financial planners do not work alone. They meet with their clients' other advisers, such as attorneys, accountants, trust officers, and investment bankers. After meeting with the clients and their advisers, financial planners analyze the data they have received and write a report detailing the clients' financial objectives, current income, investments, risk tolerance, expenses, tax returns, insurance coverage, retirement programs, estate plans, and other important information. The financial plan is a set of recommendations and strategies for clients to use or ignore, and financial planners must be ready to answer difficult questions about the plans they map out. Financial planners monitor and review plans periodically and make adjustments when necessary to ensure that each plan continues to meet the client's individual needs.

People need financial planners for different things. Some might want life insurance, college savings plans, or estate planning. Sometimes these needs are triggered by changes in people's lives, such as retirement, death of a spouse, disability, marriage, birth of children, or job changes. Financial planners devote a lot of time to investment planning, retirement planning, tax planning, estate planning, and risk management. All of these areas require different types of financial knowledge. Planners are extremely knowledgeable about asset management, employee benefits, estate planning, insurance, investments, and retirement.

Planners tailor their advice to their clients' particular needs, resources, and priorities. Many people think they cannot afford or do not need a comprehensive financial plan. Financial planners must have a certain amount of expertise in sales to build their client base. Good interpersonal skills are important for establishing solid client-planner relationships.

SCHOOL SUBJECTS
Business, Mathematics

MINIMUM EDUCATION LEVEL
Bachelor's degree

SALARY RANGE
$36,180 to $56,680 to $100,540+

OUTLOOK
Faster than the average

OTHER ARTICLES TO READ
Accountants
Business Managers
Financial Analysts
Financial Services Brokers
Tax Preparers

Financial planners develop their client lists by telephone solicitation, giving financial planning seminars to the general public or specific organizations, and networking with social and professional contacts. Referrals from satisfied customers also help business growth.

Education and Training

Financial planners need a bachelor's degree in business or science. A business administration degree with a specialization in financial planning or a liberal arts degree with courses in accounting, business administration, economics, finance, marketing, counseling, and public speaking is recommended.

Certification is available from the Certified Financial Board of the Institute of Certified Financial Planners.

Outlook

Employment of financial planners is expected to grow rapidly. There will be in-

A financial planner discusses a lifetime savings and investment plan with a young couple.

creasing demand for help with retirement-related investments and estate planning. Individual saving and investing for retirement are expected to become more important as many companies reduce pension benefits and offer investment benefits for which the employee is responsible rather than the company.

Due to the highly competitive nature of financial planning, many newcomers leave the field because they are not able to establish a sufficient clientele. Once established, however, planners can enjoy high earnings and steady work.

For More Information

Learn the terms and concepts used in the investment industry. There are hundreds of Internet sites where you can learn about financial planning. Your school or community center may have an investment club you can join. You might also ask your parents to include you in their investment planning for your college tuition.

Association for Investment Management and Research
PO Box 3668
560 Ray C. Hunt Drive
Charlottesville, VA 22903-0668
http://www.aimr.org

Certified Financial Planner Board of Standards
1670 Broadway, Suite 600
Denver, CO 80202-4809
http://www.cfp-board.org

National Association of Personal Financial Advisors
3250 North Arlington Heights Road, Suite 109
Arlington Heights, IL 60004
info@napfa.org
http://www.napfa.org

Financial Services Brokers

What Financial Services Brokers Do

Financial services brokers represent individuals and organizations in the buying and selling of stocks, bonds, and other financial products. When people buy stock, or shares, in a company, they actually own part of the company. Company managers use the money from the sale of stock to try to make the company more profitable. When the price of a stock goes up, stock owners may decide to sell their shares to make a profit. If they sell when the price has gone down, they have to take a loss. The price at any given time depends on the demand for the stock.

Financial services brokers may also be called *securities sales representatives*, *registered representatives*, *account executives*, or *stockbrokers*. They perform a variety of duties, including opening accounts for new customers. They gather certain information from customers, which is required before customers can buy and sell stocks through a stockbroker's company. The broker acts as the customer's representative, sending information to the floor of a stock exchange according to the customer's wishes to buy or sell stock.

Brokers explain the meaning of stock market terms and trading practices to customers and assess the customer's investment goals. The customer may want a short- or long-term investment. A short-term investment is usually one in which the customer has the potential to make a quick financial profit but also risks losing his or her initial investment. A long-term investment usually shows steady, slow growth. Using this information, the broker creates an individualized financial portfolio.

Financial services brokers give information to customers about the outlook on companies. They may advise customers about when to buy or sell stocks. They have to keep accurate records of all stock sales and purchases made on behalf of customers.

SCHOOL SUBJECTS
Business, Mathematics

MINIMUM EDUCATION LEVEL
Bachelor's degree

SALARY RANGE
$25,000 to $56,000 to $146,000+

OUTLOOK
Faster than the average

OTHER ARTICLES TO READ
Accountants
Business Managers
Financial Analysts
Financial Planners
Tax Preparers

Financial services brokers work for brokerage houses around the country and throughout the world. An important part of a broker's job is finding customers and building a client base. Beginning brokers spend much of their time searching for customers, relying heavily on telephone solicitation. They may also find customers through business and social contacts, or they might be given a list of likely prospects from their brokerage firm.

Education and Training

Most brokerage houses require their employees to have college degrees. Some prefer brokers with degrees in business management, economics, or finance. Employees are given on-the-job training at most brokerage houses.

Almost all states require financial services brokers to be licensed. They are sometimes given written tests. Financial services brokers also have to register as representatives of their company. This registration requires brokers to obey the rules of the stock exchange they deal with or the rules of the National Association of Securities Dealers. To become a registered representative, financial services brokers must also pass a test.

Outlook

Job opportunities for financial services brokers are expected to grow faster than the average through 2012 because of continued interest in the stock market. Many people now invest using Internet resources, and even people with limited income can invest through investment clubs, mutual funds, and monthly payment plans.

Demand for financial services brokers fluctuates with the economy. Turnover among beginners is high because they have a hard time finding enough clients. Because of potentially high earnings, competition in this business is very intense.

For More Information

Visit a local investment office, the New York Stock Exchange, or one of the commodities exchanges located in other major cities to see how transactions are handled. Join an investment club at your school or community center.

National Association of Securities Dealers
1735 K Street, NW
Washington, DC 20006
http://www.nasd.com

The Securities Industry Association
120 Broadway, 35th Floor
New York, NY 10271-0080
http://www.sia.com

Traders work on the floor of the stock exchange.

Fire Control and Safety Technicians

What Fire Control and Safety Technicians Do

Fire control and safety technicians are trained to recognize fire hazards and to prevent and control fires in homes and businesses. They work for local fire departments or for fire insurance companies, industrial organizations, government agencies, businesses that deal with fire protection equipment, and consulting services. Only a small number of firefighters are fully qualified fire control and safety technicians.

Fire control and safety technicians who work in the insurance industry examine water supply and sprinkler facilities and make recommendations for fire protection and safety measures in specific buildings. They set insurance rates, help investigate the causes of fires, and determine the amount of personal injury or property loss caused by fire.

Fire control and safety technicians in industry help plan and install prevention,

warning, and extinguishing systems and regularly inspect fire-fighting equipment such as extinguishers, hoses and hydrants, fire doors, automatic alarms, and sprinkler systems. They also point out dangerous conditions and work to improve them. They give fire safety lectures and teach employees what to do in case of a fire or other emergency.

Fire safety technicians in hotels and restaurants help prevent fires that commonly start in kitchens, laundries, and bedrooms.

Government agencies also employ fire experts to inspect government buildings, property, and storage, or develop systems for reducing fire hazards. They arrange for installations of alarm systems and fire-protection devices, formulate fire prevention plans, and assemble fire-fighting units within government agencies.

Companies that manufacture fire-protection devices and alarm systems employ technicians to explain technical functions to customers and to give advice on installation and use. They help correctly place smoke detectors and other fire prevention

---

SCHOOL SUBJECTS
Chemistry, Mathematics

MINIMUM EDUCATION LEVEL
Associate's degree

SALARY RANGE
$26,350 to $44,250 to $69,060+

OUTLOOK
About as fast as the average

OTHER ARTICLES TO READ
Emergency Medical Technicians
Fire Inspectors and Investigators
Firefighters
Health and Regulatory Inspectors
Industrial Safety and Health Technicians

or extinguishing devices, and they service fire-protection devices after installation.

Some fire control and safety technicians are involved in public education, through schools, businesses, and service clubs and organizations.

Education and Training

One way to become a fire control and safety technician is to join a local fire department as an untrained firefighter. If you are between 18 and 35 years old, in excellent physical shape, and have very good eyesight and hearing, you may be selected to train as a firefighter.

Fire control and safety technicians in business, industry, and government service must have a high school diploma and complete a two-year course in fire technology at a vocational school or community college. These programs include coursework in physics, fire-fighting tactics and strategy, fire-protection equipment and alarm systems, fundamentals of fire suppression, introductory fire technology, chemistry (especially combustion and chemistry of materials), mathematics, and communication skills.

Outlook

Technical careers in fire prevention and control are predicted to grow about as fast as the average. Technicians will find more opportunities in industry, as industries are learning that it's more affordable to hire fire protection specialists than it is to replace buildings destroyed by fire. The public's growing concern for safety and protection will also increase demand for specialists. Skilled and ambitious fire safety technicians will also be needed to monitor new

A fire control and safety inspector leads a demonstration of how to extinguish a fire in a corporate office.

fire-prevention and control techniques and technology.

For More Information

Take lifesaving and first-aid courses. Volunteer with the government park and forest service and learn about fire prevention, control, and detection. Ask a teacher or guidance counselor to arrange an interview with a firefighter and a tour of a firehouse. Volunteer for fire safety duties at your school, and learn how to operate fire extinguishers and test smoke alarms.

National Fire Academy
16825 South Seton Avenue
Emmitsburg, MD 21727
http://www.usfa.fema.gov/nfa

National Fire Protection Association
One Batterymarch Park
Quincy, MA 02169-7471
http://www.nfpa.org

Society of Fire Protection Engineers
7315 Wisconsin Avenue, Suite 620E
Bethesda, MD 20814
sfpehqtrs@sfpe.org
http://www.sfpe.org

Firefighters

SKILLS SPOTLIGHT

◆

What they do
Exercise leadership
Help clients and customers
Work with a team

What they need
Decision making
Problem solving
Responsibility

What Firefighters Do

Firefighters protect people's lives and property from the hazards of fire and other emergencies. They put out fires, rescue people from burning buildings and accident sites, and carry out safety inspections to prevent fires and unsafe conditions. Most firefighters are also trained to provide emergency medical assistance.

Emergency situations require speedy, but organized, action. Firefighters are assigned specific duties beforehand and know exactly what to do when the alarm sounds. Their tasks may be to find and rescue people, raise ladders, connect hoses to water hydrants, or break down doors or windows so that others can enter the area with water hoses. Commanding officers, such as fire captains, battalion chiefs, or the fire chief, coordinate and supervise these activities.

After a fire has been extinguished, specially trained firefighters called *arson investigators* try to find the cause of the fire. They may determine that a fire was set deliberately, gather the evidence that proves this and provides clues as to who set the fire, arrest the suspected arsonist, and testify in court.

Firefighters often answer calls requesting emergency medical care, such as help in giving artificial respiration to drowning victims or aid to heart attack victims. They sometimes provide emergency medical treatment after natural disasters, such as earthquakes and tornadoes, as well as man-made disasters, such as oil spills and other hazardous chemical incidents, or rescuing victims of bombings.

Between alarm calls, firefighters keep the fire-fighting equipment in good shape. They polish and lubricate mechanical equipment, dry and stretch hoses into shape, and repair their protective gear. They hold practice drills to improve their fire-fighting procedures.

Firefighters often work long shifts, spending many hours at a time in the station. They are prepared to answer an alarm call at any moment. In many smaller towns, firefighters may be employed on a part-time basis or serve as volunteers. This means that they are on alarm call from their homes, and sometimes they have to

SCHOOL SUBJECTS
Biology, Chemistry

MINIMUM EDUCATION LEVEL
High school diploma

SALARY RANGE
$21,000 to $43,000 to $78,000

OUTLOOK
As fast as the average

OTHER ARTICLES TO READ
Emergency Medical Technicians
Fire Control and Safety Technicians
Fire Inspectors and Investigators
Industrial Safety and Health Technicians

Firefighters spray water on a burning building.

leave during a family meal or in the middle of the night.

Education and Training

In most towns and cities, firefighters must have a high school education. Some cities require associate's or bachelor's degrees. Applicants usually must pass written tests and meet certain requirements for height, weight, physical fitness, stamina, and vision. Firefighters must be at least 18 years old.

Many junior and community colleges offer two-year postsecondary school fire technology programs. These programs include courses in physics and hydraulics as they apply to pump and nozzle pressure, fundamentals of chemistry, and communications.

Beginning firefighters receive several weeks of intensive training, either on the job or through formal fire department training schools. This training covers fundamentals of city laws and ordinances, fire prevention, first aid, and the use and care of equipment.

Outlook

Employment of firefighters is expected to grow about as fast as the average through 2012. The field is extremely competitive, and the number of people interested in becoming firefighters will be greater than the number of available positions in most areas.

Most new jobs will be created as small communities grow and add career firefighters to their volunteer staffs. There are also growing numbers of "call" firefighters, who are paid only when they respond to fires. Some local governments are expected to contract for fire-fighting services with private companies.

For More Information

To learn more, take first aid and cardio-pulmonary resuscitation courses offered by the American Red Cross, or a community organization. You can also volunteer for any fire prevention activities offered at your school.

International Association of Fire Fighters
1750 New York Avenue, NW
Washington, DC 20006
http://www.iaff.org

National Fire Protection Association
One Batterymarch Park
Quincy, MA 02169-7471
http://www.nfpa.org

Fire Inspectors and Investigators

SKILLS SPOTLIGHT

◆

What they do
Communicate ideas
Evaluate and manage information
Help clients and customers

Skills they need
Decision making
Problem solving
Speaking/listening

What Fire Inspectors and Investigators Do

Most fire departments are responsible for fire prevention activities. *Fire inspectors* inspect buildings and their storage contents for trash, rubbish, chemicals, and other materials that can ignite easily. They look for worn-out or exposed wiring and electrical code violations. Fire inspectors also examine a facility's fire protection equipment, such as sprinkler systems, alarms, and fire extinguishers, to make sure all systems are functioning properly. While inspecting buildings, they may recommend better placement or use of fire-safety equipment. They provide information regarding the storage of flammable materials, electrical hazards, and other common causes of fires.

Fire inspectors pay close attention to public buildings, such as hospitals, schools, nursing homes, theaters, restaurants, and hotels, which they inspect regularly. They also review evacuation plans and monitor fire drills to make sure the plans are effective.

Inspectors review plans for new buildings to make sure they incorporate fire suppression and alarm systems that are adequate and conform to government safety codes.

Inspectors maintain a variety of reports and records related to fire inspections, code requirements, permits, and training. They also instruct employers, civic groups, schoolchildren, and others on extinguishing small fires, escaping burning buildings, operating fire extinguishers, and establishing evacuation plans.

Fire investigators, or *fire marshals,* try to find the causes of fires. Once fires are extinguished, investigators determine the fuel and heat sources that cause the fires. They determine whether the fire was arson, meaning deliberately set, or accidental. If the fires are of suspicious origin or caused death or injury, investigators look for more evidence of arson. Fire investigators interrogate witnesses, obtain statements and other documentation, and preserve and examine

SCHOOL SUBJECTS
Biology, Chemistry, Physics

MINIMUM EDUCATION LEVEL
Some postsecondary training

SALARY RANGE
$29,000 to $46,000 to $71,000+

OUTLOOK
About as fast as the average

OTHER ARTICLES TO READ
Fire Control and Safety Technicians
Firefighters
Health and Regulatory Inspectors
Park Rangers

Two fire inspectors check a boiler room for potential fire hazards.

evidence. They tour fire scenes and prepare comprehensive reports of investigative procedures.

Fire investigators submit reports to a district attorney, testify in court, or, if they have police authority, arrest suspected arsonists. Investigators also gather information from accidental fires to determine where and how the fire started and how it spread.

Education and Training

There are two ways to become a fire inspector. Some fire departments have policies that only those who have served as firefighters can work in the fire prevention bureau. Other departments want people who are trained primarily for fire prevention. Either way, if you want to join the fire department, you should take a two- or four-year college program in fire service, fire protection, and fire-protection systems and equipment. Specialized fire prevention classes required for inspectors, such as hazardous materials and processes, flammable liquids, and high-piled stock, are offered by colleges or the state fire marshal's office.

Fire investigators must have knowledge of fire science, chemistry, engineering, and investigative techniques. A law enforcement background is also helpful.

Outlook

The outlook for fire inspectors is about the same as for firefighters. Employment should grow about as fast as the average for all occupations through 2012. Fire investigators have a slightly better employment outlook than fire inspectors, since, unfortunately, there will always be fires to investigate. This field is constantly being advanced by new technology and remains one of the most interesting aspects of the fire service.

For More Information

Become familiar with fire safety and science by visiting the fire safety and education section of the U.S. Fire Administration Web site, http://www.usfa.fema.gov/safety. Also visit the U.S. Fire Administration's main Web page at http://www.usfa.fema.gov.

International Association of Arson Investigators
12770 Boenker Road
Bridgeton, MO 63044
http://www.firearson.com

National Fire Academy
16825 South Seton Avenue
Emmitsburg, MD 21727
http://www.usfa.fema.gov/nfa

National Fire Protection Association
One Batterymarch Park
Quincy, MA 02169-7471
http://www.nfpa.org

Fishers

What Fishers Do

Fishers catch fish and other sea life and sell it to restaurants, fish markets, and other businesses. Fishers are grouped according to the equipment they use, the fish they catch, and where they catch the fish.

Fishers may work alone in small boats or with crews of as many as 25 people in a group of boats called a fleet. They can remain at sea for several days or for months at a time. Most commercial fishing is done in distant ocean waters. Only a small percentage of fish are caught in rivers, streams, ponds, or lakes, or harvested from fish farms.

Net fishers catch fish with nets. They are the largest group of fishers and catch most of the world's supply of fish. They mainly use three types of nets: seines, trawls, and gill nets. Fishing crews use seines to catch schools of herring, mackerel, sardines, tuna, and other fish that swim near the surface. Trawls are funnel-shaped nets used to catch shrimp, cod, scallops, and other shellfish on or near the ocean floor. Fishers use sonar before they drop these nets to find the greatest number of fish. Only a small number of fishers use the gill net, which acts like a wall, entangling fish such as salmon, sharks, and herring.

Line fishers catch fish with poles, hooks, and lines. They work alone or in crews, laying out lines and attaching hooks, bait, and other equipment, depending on the type of fish they plan to catch. They then lower these lines into the water. To haul catches on board they use reels, winches, or their bare hands.

Pot fishers trap crab, lobster, and eel in cages containing bait. Some chase turtles and certain kinds of fish into net traps. They fish near the shore or in inland waters off small boats. Pot fishers lower the cages into the water, pulling them in when the fish is trapped, and dumping the catch onto the deck.

Some fishers focus on recreation, operating fishing vessels for sport fishing, socializing, and relaxation.

Education and Training

Fishers learn their trade on the job. Some high schools, colleges, and technical schools offer courses in handling boats, fishing equipment, navigation, and meteorology. Postsecondary schools provide information on electronic navigation and communications equipment and fishing gear.

Captains and first mates on large fishing vessels of at least 200 gross tons must be licensed. Captains of charter sport fishing boats must also be licensed, regardless of the size of the vessel.

Outlook

The fishing industry has experienced hard times in the past few decades, and employment for fishers is expected to decline through 2012. The industry is affected by environmental law, ship maintenance costs, improvements in electronic and other fishing gear (which has limited the expansion in crew size), and the increasing use of "floating processors," which process catches on-board, further limiting employment opportunities. However, new technology also helps the industry: super-chilled refrigerator hulls help keep fish fresh for higher selling prices, and color monitors help fishers see nets and fish while still under water.

Pollution and excessive fishing have decreased the fish stock, particularly in the North Atlantic and Pacific Northwest. Some states have limited the number of fishing permits to allow regrowth of fish and shellfish populations.

For More Information

If you live on the coast, find work on a small fishing boat or at a fishing port. Contact a state department of fish and game to learn more about the local fishing industry.

A lobsterman examines his catch off the coast of Quahog Bay, Maine.

Working at a fish market can acquaint you with different kinds of fish and consumer demand for seafood.

National Marine Fisheries Service
NOAA Fisheries Headquarters
1315 East-West Highway, 9th Floor
Silver Spring, MD 20910
http://www.nmfs.noaa.gov

National Oceanic and Atmospheric Administration
14th Street and Constitution Avenue, NW
Room 6217
Washington, DC 20230
202-482-6090
http://www.noaa.gov

Fitness Directors

What Fitness Directors Do

Fitness directors organize and schedule exercise classes and programs for health clubs, resorts, cruise lines, corporations, and other institutions. They work with other fitness professionals, such as personal trainers, nutritionists, and health care personnel, to deliver the best services for the individuals who use the fitness facility. Fitness directors must balance the needs of their staff with the needs of the paying customers. They accomplish this task by listening and responding to feedback from staff and clients regarding program changes or additions, instructor criticisms, and any other comments concerning programs, staff, and the facility.

Fitness directors are a crucial part of sports and health facilities. They hire and manage exercise instructors and personal trainers for their facility. In addition, they coordinate the schedules of exercise instructors and personal trainers. They also make sure that their institution offers a wide variety of options to keep different customers content. For example, a fitness director who works at an elder assisted living or nursing home must plan and direct classes that appeal to the varying abilities of an older population. Similarly, a fitness director who works on a cruise ship must balance the scheduling and programming desires of parents and children.

Directors must also be observant about health and safety issues in their facilities. For example, fitness directors ensure that equipment and rooms are clean, exercise machines are operating correctly, and the temperature of rooms is comfortable.

Fitness directors must have excellent organizational and leadership skills to plan activities, manage staff, and respond effectively to customer suggestions, complaints, and desires.

Education and Training

If you are interested in working in a health and fitness facility, take science and physical education classes and get involved in sports activities. It is also important to take home economics classes, which include lessons in diet and nutrition. Business courses can help

SCHOOL SUBJECTS
Health, Physical education

MINIMUM EDUCATION LEVEL
Some postsecondary training

SALARY RANGE
$19,000 to $30,000 to $53,000

OUTLOOK
Much faster than the average

OTHER ARTICLES TO READ
Aerobics Instructors
Athletic Directors
Athletic Trainers
Yoga and Pilates Instructors

A fitness director at a gym speaks with clients after a kickboxing class.

you prepare for the management aspect of the job.

Fitness directors should have a background in exercise science to be able to serve their clients and understand the needs of their fitness facility. Associate and bachelor's degree programs in health education, exercise and sports science, fitness program management, and athletic training are offered in colleges all over the country and highly recommended in order to obtain a director position.

Certification in fitness or exercise science is also highly recommended and often required to work in a management-level position at a fitness facility. Some employers also require that their fitness staff members be certified in cardiopulmonary resuscitation (CPR).

Outlook

Employment of all fitness workers, including fitness directors, is expected to increase much faster than the average through 2012. This is largely due to the rapidly growing interest of Americans to engage in personal training, aerobics instruction, and other fitness activities designed to maintain a healthy lifestyle and a fit physique. Employers are also increasingly promoting exercise to improve the good health and productivity of their workers.

Job opportunities for fitness directors should be widely available at health clubs, gyms, corporate fitness centers, day care centers, nursing homes, resorts, and cruise lines. Previous experience as a personal trainer, aerobics instructor, or physical therapist is often quite helpful.

For More Information

If your school offers exercise classes or some other after-school fitness program, sign up and note what you like and dislike about instructor methods or the environment. If there is an affordable gym or health club in your community, take a tour and even a sample class or two. While at the facility, talk to an instructor, manager, or trainer about his or her job and work environment and learn how he or she got started in the industry.

Aerobics and Fitness Association of America
15250 Ventura Boulevard, Suite 200
Sherman Oaks, CA 91403-3297
877-968-7263
http://www.afaa.com

American Council on Exercise
4851 Paramount Drive
San Diego, CA 92123
800-825-3636
conted@acefitness.org
http://www.acefitness.org

Medical Fitness Association
PO Box 73103
Richmond, VA 23235-8026
804-327-0330
info@medicafitness.org
http://www.medicalfitness.org

Flight Attendants

What Flight Attendants Do

Flight attendants provide a variety of services to make airplane passengers comfortable during flights. They may serve on flights traveling several hundred miles within the United States or on international flights traveling thousands of miles around the world.

Before takeoff, flight attendants attend a briefing session with the rest of the flight crew. They carefully check flight supplies, life jackets, oxygen masks, and other passenger safety equipment. They make sure passenger cabins are neat and furnished with pillows and blankets. They also check the plane galley, to see that food and beverages are on board and that all is secure for takeoff.

Attendants welcome the passengers and check their tickets as they board the plane. They show passengers where to store their belongings and direct them to their seats. They often give special attention to elderly or disabled passengers and people traveling with small children.

Before takeoff, a flight attendant speaks to the passengers, usually over a loudspeaker. He or she introduces the crew and flight attendants, and discusses the weather, altitude, and safety information. As required by federal law, flight attendants demonstrate the use of lifesaving equipment and safety procedures.

From takeoff to landing, flight attendants routinely check to make sure passengers are wearing their safety belts properly and have their seats in an upright position. They may distribute reading materials to passengers and answer questions regarding flight schedules or the geographic terrain over which the plane is passing. They observe passengers during the flight to ensure their comfort, assisting anyone who becomes ill or nervous.

Attendants may serve prepared meals or refreshments. They are also responsible for filling out passenger reports and issuing boarding passes. Attendants on international flights may provide customs and airport information and sometimes translate flight information or passenger instructions into a foreign language.

Education and Training

Airlines in the United States require flight attendants to be U.S. citizens, and have permanent resident status or valid work visas. Applicants must be at least 18 to 21 years old, although some airlines have higher minimum age requirements. There are height and weight requirements as well.

Many airlines prefer flight attendants to have college degrees, although it is not a requirement. All potential attendants attend training programs offered by airlines or private schools to learn about company operations and schedules, flight regulations and duties, first aid, grooming, emergency operations and evacuation procedures, flight terminology, and public relations. Flight attendants receive additional emergency and passenger procedures training each year. Trainees for international flights are instructed on customs and visa regulations, as well as procedures to follow in the event of terrorist attacks. New attendants serve a six-month probationary period, after which they are assigned regular flights if their work is acceptable.

Outlook

Employment opportunities for flight attendants will grow about as fast as the average through 2012. The terrorist attacks of 2001 impacted the airlines industry, and several thousand flight attendants were laid off. The industry is recovering, though, as passengers are feeling more comfortable traveling by air.

The flight attendant field is highly competitive and turnover is not as high as

Flight attendants work to make the passengers' flight as comfortable as possible.

it once was. Job applicants with two years of college and prior customer relations experience will have an advantage.

For More Information

Airline companies and private training schools have brochures describing the flight attendant field. A customer service job, such as in food service, hospitality, or retail sales, is a good introduction to the kind of work flight attendants do.

Air Transport Association of America Inc.
1301 Pennsylvania Avenue, NW, Suite 1100
Washington, DC 20004-1707
ata@airlines.org
http://www.airlines.org

Association of Flight Attendants–CWA
501 Third Street, NW
Washington, DC 20001
http://www.afanet.org

U.S. Department of Transportation
Federal Aviation Administration
800 Independence Avenue, SW
Washington, DC 20591
http://www.faa.gov

Flight Instructors

What Flight Instructors Do

Flight instructors are pilots who use their experience, knowledge, joy of flying, and ability to explain complex subjects to teach students how to fly aircraft. Flight instructors give classroom as well as hands-on flying instruction to their students. Topics covered include aerodynamics, navigation, instrument reading, aircraft control techniques, and federal aviation regulations. They may teach at flight schools, for airlines, in the military, in a university, or work as self-employed instructors. Although flight instructors fly with students, it is the instructor who is ultimately responsible for making sure all appropriate preflight, in-flight, and postlanding procedures are followed.

Instructors must know current federal aviation regulations so that they can teach correct rules to their students. Flight instructors should also be up to date on the latest teaching technologies available. Computer-based programs and flight simulators, for example, are often used in flight instruction, and instructors should be able to make use of these resources.

Taking students on training flights is another important part of a flight instructor's work. Flight instructors also teach students how to maintain a flight logbook. Each student must record information about the flights he or she makes, such as what was done on the flight, how long the flight took, and the flight's distance. In addition, instructors need to keep their own "teacher's logbook" with information on each student.

In order to get the student pilot certificate, the student must pass a test given by the flight instructor. After a student passes this test, the instructor continues to work with students until the students complete all their training and get their FAA (Federal Aeronautics Association) pilot's certificate or license.

Flight instructors are only allowed to teach the categories for which they are already certified. Consequently, instructors are often students themselves, learning to operate different aircraft and getting various certifications.

SCHOOL SUBJECTS
Mathematics, Physics

MINIMUM EDUCATION LEVEL
Some postsecondary training

SALARY RANGE
$42,000 to $128,000 to $146,000

OUTLOOK
About as fast as the average

OTHER ARTICLES TO READ
Adult and Vocational Education Teachers
Aircraft Mechanics
Air Traffic Controllers
Flight Attendants
Pilots

Education and Training

Chemistry, physics, algebra, geometry, computer science, and other advanced science and math classes are important to take in high school and college. To help you develop your teaching skills, take English, psychology, or communications classes.

Although the FAA does not require flight instructors to have a particular degree, a college education is highly recommended. You may want to attend a university with a specialized aviation program, such as the Institute of Aviation at the University of Illinois-Urbana Champaign. If you prefer, though, you can take a broader course of study at any college, join the military to obtain flight training, obtain private lessons, or enroll in a flight school.

To become a flight instructor, you will need to get FAA flight-instructor certification. To do this, you must have a commercial pilot's certification for the kind of aircraft (single engine, multi-engine, instrument, and so on) that matches the flight instructor rating (designation) you want to have.

Outlook

The U.S. Department of Labor estimates that job growth for all types of pilots, including flight instructors, will be at an average rate through 2012. However, the growth rate depends a great deal on both the pilot's specific occupation and the overall condition of the economy. Additionally, instructors who are working will be more likely to keep those jobs than to move into other positions and make way for new flight instructors.

This flight instructor accompanies a student during a lesson.

For More Information

You can explore aspects of this field while you are still in middle school. Begin by reading aviation magazines as well as studying materials covering topics such as aviation weather, aeronautical knowledge, and weight and balance. You can also begin developing radio skills by learning to use a ham radio.

EAA Air Academy
PO Box 3086
Oshkosh, WI 54903-3086
888-322-3229
http://www.eaa.org/education/airacademy.html

Federal Aviation Administration
800 Independence Avenue, SW, Room 810
Washington, DC 20591
202-366-4000
http://www.faa.gov

National Association of Flight Instructors
EAA Aviation Center
PO Box 3086
Oshkosh, WI 54902-6649
920-426-6801
nafi@eaa.org
http://www.nafinet.org

Floor Covering Installers

What Floor Covering Installers Do

Floor covering installers lay down carpets, tiles, and other floor covering material. They work in almost every kind of construction project. Installers either replace or repair worn floor coverings in public buildings or private homes, or they install floors in new buildings.

Some installers specialize in laying tiles and vinyl sheets or carpets, while others work with all types of surfaces. Before laying the covering, installers inspect the floor to determine its condition. The floor must be dry, smooth, and free of loose dust or dirt. The installer may sweep, sand, or scrape dirt from the floor and fill cracks with a filler material.

When the layout is clear, installers measure and cut the covering to create proper-sized sections. They also cut and lay foundation materials, such as felt, on the sub-floor. With chalk lines and dividers, installers place guidelines on the foundation material. They trowel on adhesive cement and lay the floor covering in place, following the guidelines. Installers are especially careful to align the pieces if there is any pattern in the flooring. They also pay attention to fitting pieces into odd-shaped areas around door openings, pipes, and posts. They use a roller to smooth the covering into place, ensuring good adhesion.

Carpet layers measure floors and plan the layout, allowing for foot-traffic patterns and placing seams where they will be least noticed. Carpet is stretched and fastened into place and then nailed to strips along the border of the floor or directly to the floor itself. Carpet layers may sew seams with a curved needle and special thread or use a heat-activated adhesive tape and an electric heating tool.

Installers work with ordinary hand tools, such as mallets, staple guns, pry bars, trowels, knives, shears, hammers, drills, and tape measures, and a variety of special tools, such as stretching devices and floor rollers.

Education and Training

Floor covering installers must be able to read blueprints and sketches and follow instructions carefully. They must be good at working with all types of construction materials (wood, plywood, and cement) and using the proper methods for fastening carpets, tile, or vinyl to these surfaces. Installers need to be skilled in using hand tools, power tools, and measuring devices.

The best way to become a floor covering installer is to learn the skills on the job as a helper to an experienced installer or through a formal apprenticeship program, which includes on-the-job training as well as classroom instruction.

Helpers begin with simple tasks, such as stretching newly installed carpet, and they gradually take on more difficult assignments, such as measuring, cutting, and fitting material. A high school diploma is preferred, though not always necessary.

Outlook

Employment of floor covering installers is expected to increase at an average rate through 2012. Carpet installers should have the best employment opportunities. Most job opportunities will open as a result of experienced workers leaving the field or retiring.

Even during economic downturns, when new construction levels drop, jobs for installers should remain steady because of the ongoing need to renovate existing buildings.

A floor covering installer installs indoor/outdoor carpeting on a front porch.

For More Information

Take part in a home improvement project, such as installing vinyl floor tiles or laying carpet. Any type of construction project will help you learn about reading plans, measuring, cutting different materials, applying adhesives, and using hand tools.

The Carpet and Rug Institute
PO Box 2048
Dalton, GA 30722-2048
http://www.carpet-rug.com

Floor Covering Installation Contractors Association
7439 Millwood Drive
West Bloomfield, MI 48322-1234
info@fcica.com
http://www.fcica.com

World Floor Covering Association
2211 East Howell Avenue
Anaheim, CA 92806
http://www.wfca.org

Florists

What Florists Do

Florists work with decorative flowers and plants. Some florists work in greenhouses or on farms, overseeing flowers and plants that will be sold to flower shops.

Many flowers and plants are delicate and need special care. Florists know what kind of care to give each type of flower or plant. They make sure that the plants they grow receive proper water, food, and light. They decide when to plant or transplant flower crops and when to cut or harvest them. They cut and bundle flowers or plants so that they can be sold to flower shops.

Another type of florist is a *floral designer*. Floral designers usually work in flower shops or in floral departments of grocery stores, or they may work independently. Floral designers cut and arrange live, dried, or artificial flowers and plants. They may make bouquets, wreaths, corsages, centerpieces, or terrariums.

Floral designers usually work from a written order. Orders include the price of the arrangement and the date, time, and place of delivery. Sometimes the orders include the types or colors of flowers to use, and sometimes the florist makes those decisions.

To choose flowers for an arrangement, florists look for colors and shapes that work well together. They also think about which kinds of flowers or plants will work best for the arrangement they are creating. Some flowers are more expensive than others, so florists must always consider the price of an arrangement when choosing materials for it.

Along with live flowers, designers may use silk flowers or foliage, fresh fruit and twigs, or incorporate decorative items such as candles and stuffed animals in their arrangements. They use foam, wire, wooden or plastic picks, shears, florist's knife, tape, and a variety of containers. Techniques such as wiring flower stems or shading the tips of blooms with paint or glitter are often used to give floral arrangements a finished look.

Many floral designers specialize in weddings and other large-scale special events that take months of planning. Such events require florists to design arrangements;

In preparation for a wedding, this florist must busily work to arrange centerpieces and bouquets for the bride and her six attendants.

order flowers and supplies; and produce, deliver, and place decorations. These may include altar or church decorations, bouquets, corsages, boutonnieres, and table centerpieces. Since flowers must be freshly cut to last during an event, floral designers work long and frenzied hours just before the special day.

Education and Training

Many florists learn their skills by working as assistants or apprentices to experienced designers. Most designers today, however, complete a floral design certificate or degree program.

The American Floral Art School, a state-approved and licensed vocational school in Chicago, offers certificates in modern floral design. Many universities also offer degrees in floriculture and horticulture, and community colleges and independent schools offer certification in floral design.

Outlook

Floral design is expected to grow about as fast as the average for all other occupations through 2012. Even small towns have at least one flower shop. Grocery stores now have full-service floral departments, and there are even international floral wire services, such as Amlings, FTD, and Teleflora. Floral experts who are able to create exciting and original designs will be in high demand. Certified designers may have an edge for the best jobs.

For More Information

Community centers, arts and crafts stores, gardening centers, and vocational schools may offer workshops in floral design. Study books on flowers and plants to learn about flower varieties, growing seasons and conditions, harvesting, and floral design techniques.

American Institute of Floral Designers
720 Light Street
Baltimore, MD 21230
410-752-3318
http://www.aifd.org

Rittners School of Floral Design
345 Marlborough Street
Boston, MA 02115
617-267-3824
http://www.floralschool.com

Society of American Florists
1601 Duke Street
Alexandria, VA 22314
800-336-4743
http://www.safnow.org

Fluid Power Technicians

What Fluid Power Technicians Do

Fluid power technicians work with machines powered by the pressure of a liquid or gas in a closed container. Many machines need some kind of fluid power system to operate. These fluid-powered machines are used in manufacturing, agriculture, and defense and in such everyday devices as automatic doors, machines for inflating tires, brakes, steering, and transmissions of vehicles.

There are two types of fluid power systems. Hydraulic machines use water, oil, or another liquid in a closed system to transmit energy. For example, a hydraulic jack, which is used to lift heavy loads, is a cylinder with a piston fitted inside it. When a liquid is pumped into the bottom of the cylinder, the piston is forced upward, lifting the weight on the jack. To lower the weight, the liquid is released through a valve, returning the pressure to normal.

Pneumatic machines use another type of fluid power system. Pressure from air or gas in a closed system activates these machines.

Pavement-breaking jackhammers and compressed-air paint sprayers are common examples of pneumatic machines.

Fluid power systems are a part of most machines used in industry, so technicians work in many different environments. Most often, they work in factories where fluid-power systems are used in manufacturing. For example, they maintain and service pneumatic machines that bolt products together on an assembly line.

Fluid power technicians generally work under the supervision of engineers or an engineering team. They use hand tools, electronic testing devices, blueprints, technical manuals, and computer printouts to assemble, repair, and test the fluid power equipment.

Some technicians work in laboratories on research and development teams that are looking for better ways to use fluid power systems. Other technicians work for companies that make and sell fluid power equipment to industrial plants. These technicians travel from one plant to another, providing customers with specialized information and

SCHOOL SUBJECTS
Mathematics
Technical/shop

MINIMUM EDUCATION LEVEL
Some postsecondary training

SALARY RANGE
$35,000 to $40,000 to $50,000+

OUTLOOK
About as fast as the average

OTHER ARTICLES TO READ
Agribusiness Technicians
Aircraft Mechanics
Automobile Mechanics
Industrial Machinery Mechanics

A fluid power technician checks a valve for defects.

assistance. Some technicians repair and maintain fluid power components of heavy equipment used in construction, farming, or mining. Because fluid power technology is important to airplane controls, landing gear, and brakes, many technicians are employed in the aircraft industry.

Education and Training

Courses in computer science and mathematics, especially geometry and algebra, are helpful in this field. Physical science, as well as shop and English, are also recommended.

Most employers prefer to hire fluid power technicians who have at least two years of postsecondary training in programs offered by community colleges and technical institutes. Very few of those programs, however, include fluid power technology. Training in a related field, such as mechanical or electrical technology, is often acceptable.

Outlook

Many different industries use fluid power, so the need for technicians is growing rapidly. Currently, there are not enough technicians to meet the demand. Electrohydraulic and electropneumatic technologies have opened up new markets, such as active suspensions on automobiles, and reestablished older markets, such as robotics. Therefore, the fluid power industry is expected to continue growing, and the outlook for technicians should remain strong through the next decade.

For More Information

Your school or public library has books that explain fluid power. Take classes in machine shop, physics, or electronics offered at your school, community center, or vocational school. Join a science club that might give you the opportunity to work on machines, such as robots.

Fluid Power Educational Foundation
3333 North Mayfair Road, Suite 211
Milwaukee, WI 53222
http://www.fpef.org

Fluid Power Society
PO Box 1420
Cherry Hill, NJ 08034
info@ifps.org
http://www.ifps.org

National Fluid Power Association
3333 North Mayfair Road
Milwaukee, WI 53222-3219
nfpa@nfpa.com
http://www.nfpa.com

Food Photographers

SKILLS SPOTLIGHT

◆

What they do
Communicate ideas
Select and apply tools/technology
Work with a team

Skills they need
Creative thinking
Decision making
Self-management

What Food Photographers Do

Food photographers work hard to make their viewers crave a dish without the help of the food's appealing presence, taste, aroma, and texture. They create and capture these beautiful and enticing images of food for magazines, cookbooks, and restaurant promotional materials. They work with food stylists to make the food look as appetizing and aesthetically beautiful as possible.

Food photographers must set up shoots with clients and decide on the look of the shot. Once a date is set, the photographer has to make sure all the props are ordered and that he or she has enough help for the shoot. The photographer or the client may hire food stylists, camera assistants, and prop movers to aid in the shoot.

A lot of extra care and time has to go into the preparation and styling of the food. While the food stylist designs the food and places it on the proper plate, platter, or other background, the food photographer selects and organizes the cameras, lighting, and props of the shoot. Sometimes food "stand-ins" are utilized and chemical treatments are applied to foods to preserve a fresh and appealing look.

Once the shot is fully set up and the client is happy with the look, the photo subject, called the "hero dish," is brought in, and pictures are taken quickly to make sure the food remains looking fresh and appealing.

Many food photographers work as freelancers, contracting work out to others. Those who do this usually spend the majority of the time *not* shooting film, but running all aspects of their business.

Education and Training

Art, cooking, math, chemistry, and other science classes will help familiarize you with different foods, assist in the development of a better "eye" for detail, and provide you with knowledge about the technical aspects of food preparation and photography. You should also be sure to take computer science classes and explore software that can store

SCHOOL SUBJECTS
Art, Family and consumer science

MINIMUM EDUCATION LEVEL
Some postsecondary training

SALARY RANGE
$15,000 to $26,000 to $54,000

OUTLOOK
About as fast as the average

OTHER ARTICLES TO READ
Cooks, Chefs, and Bakers
Photo Editors
Photographers
Photography Instructors
Photojournalists
Photo Stylists

and manipulate images, such as Adobe PhotoShop and Illustrator.

Professional postsecondary training programs will help you get the experience and skills necessary to land a job or attract clients. A culinary degree program that provides a background knowledge of photography will ensure that you know how to prepare foods and are familiar with their different chemical properties. Those who choose to enter photography programs will be well versed in the technical side of photography and may even be able to take some specialty classes in food photography.

Outlook

Employment of all photographers will increase about as fast as the average for all occupations through 2012. Job prospects for food photographers depend heavily on the overall health of the food and entertainment industries. Though many companies have reduced their advertising budgets, they still have to employ professionals to capture images of their food for print and Web advertising. Most restaurants, no matter how successful, will need to display their food in menus or ads to attract diners.

It is important to note, however, that though there will always be jobs for food photographers, the field is incredibly competitive. Only those with the right blend of technical and business skills will be able to find enough work to shoot pictures full time.

For More Information

While in school, be sure to get involved in clubs that will help you explore your interests and skills in cooking and photography.

Here, a food photographer has photographed an individual raspberry trifle for use in a desserts cookbook.

If you have a camera and some film, take test shots of kitchen and food items, paying attention to how different lighting and props affect the result of the picture.

American Society of Media Photographers
150 North Second Street
Philadelphia, PA 19106
215-451-2767
http://www.asmp.org

Culinary Institute of America
1946 Campus Drive
Hyde Park, NY 12538-1499
800-285-4627
careers@culinary.edu
http://www.ciachef.edu

Professional Photographers of America
229 Peachtree Street, NE, Suite 2200
Atlanta, GA 30303
404-522-8600
csc@ppa.com
http://www.ppa.com

Food Production Workers

What Food Production Workers Do

Food production workers are responsible for the steps involved in manufacturing mass-produced foods, such as baked goods, candy, dairy products, canned goods, beverages, and pasta.

Bakery workers produce bread, cakes, biscuits, pies, pastries, crackers, and other baked goods in commercial, institutional, and industrial bakeries. *Batchmakers* are employed in manufacturing settings to tend equipment that mixes, blends, and cooks, and *bakers* work in such places as grocery stores, specialty shops, and manufacturing.

Beverage industry workers manufacture and bottle or package soft drinks, including carbonated beverages, coffee, tea, juices, and more recently, mineral and spring waters, also called "designer waters."

Canning and preserving industry workers monitor equipment and perform routine tasks to can, preserve, and quick-freeze such foods as vegetables, fruits, frozen dinners, jams, jellies, preserves, pickles, and soups. They also process and preserve seafood, including shrimp, oysters, crabs, clams, and fish.

Confectionery industry workers manufacture and package sweets, including bonbons, hard and soft candy, stuffed dates, popcorn balls, and many other types of confections.

Dairy products workers set up, operate, and tend continuous-flow or vat-type equipment to process milk, cream, butter, cheese, ice cream, and other dairy products, following specified methods and formulas.

Meat packing workers slaughter, clean, cut, process, and package the meat from cattle, hogs, sheep, and poultry. They also process animal parts for by-products such as margarine, lard, animal feed, and non-food products, such as fertilizer, hides, and soap.

Food production workers also work in kitchens of large institutions, such as hospitals and schools. They prepare large quantities of foods that will be served cafeteria style or on trays to patients.

SCHOOL SUBJECTS
Family and consumer science,
   Mathematics

MINIMUM EDUCATION LEVEL
High school diploma

SALARY RANGE
$14,0000 to $22,000 to $36,000

OUTLOOK
As fast as the average

OTHER ARTICLES TO READ
Cooks, Chefs, and Bakers
Food Service Workers
Food Technologists
Meat Packers and Meat Cutters

Tending ovens and other equipment can be very hot. Some industrial food machines are noisy, and certain positions may require heavy lifting. In some large bakeries, workers are needed for evening and night shifts, or they may have to begin work very early in the morning.

Food production workers must ensure that food items are processed in a completely sanitary manner up to company and government standards. Accuracy is required in measuring and mixing ingredients and in following instructions. Manual dexterity and physical strength are also useful in many food productions jobs.

Education and Training

A high school diploma is usually required for food production workers. Classes in chemistry, biology, and machine shop might be helpful, although specific production skills can be learned only on the job.

For some food production jobs, such as bakery workers, it takes many years to become an expert. A good way to become a skilled baker is to enroll as a baker's apprentice. An apprenticeship lasts three to four years and includes classroom instruction and on-the-job training.

Many food production careers are available for laboratory, engineering, and supervisory workers. These positions often require a bachelor's or master's degree.

Outlook

The food industry is the largest single industry in the United States and throughout the world. There will always be a need for people to process food products. However, the use of automated equipment and computer technology throughout the food-pro-

Food production workers must work quickly and efficiently, but they also must make sure that every detail is perfect.

cessing industry means that fewer people will be needed to process, preserve, and can foods by hand.

For More Information

Take cooking classes, and practice cooking for and serving your family. Volunteer for food preparation jobs at community centers, shelters, and social service agencies that serve meals to the needy.

Food Products Association
1350 I Street, NW, Suite 300
Washington, DC 20005
202-639-5900
http://www.fpa-food.org

Institute of Food Technologists
525 West Van Buren, Suite 1000
Chicago, IL 60607
312-782-8424
http://www.ift.org

Glossary

Accredited Meets established standards for providing good training and education. Usually given by an independent organization of professionals to a school or a program in a school. Compare **certified** and **licensed.**

Apprentice A person who is learning a trade by working under the supervision of a skilled worker. Often receive classroom instruction in addition to their supervised practical experience.

Apprenticeship 1. A program for training apprentices (see apprentice). 2. The period of time that a person is working as an apprentice, usually three or four years.

Associate degree An academic rank or title given to a person who has completed a two-year program of study at a community college, junior college, or similar institution.

Bachelor's degree An academic rank or title given to a person who has completed a four-year program of study at a college or university. Also called an undergraduate degree or baccalaureate.

Certified Meets established requirements for skill, knowledge, and experience in a particular field. Granted by organizations of professionals in their field. Compare **accredited** and **licensed.**

Commission A percentage of sales revenue that is given to the salesperson as pay, either in addition to or instead of a salary.

Community college A public two-year college that grants an associate degree. Graduates may transfer to a four-year college or university to complete a bachelor's degree. Compare **junior college** and **technical community college.**

Curriculum All the courses available in a school within a particular subject.

Degree An academic distinction given by a college or university to a student who has completed a program of study.

Diploma A certificate or document given by a school to show that a person has completed a course of study or has graduated from the school.

Doctorate (Ph.D.) The highest-level academic rank or title granted by a graduate school to a person who has completed a two- to three-year program of study at a university after receiving a master's degree.

Downsizing To reduce in size or number. Often used in the business world to describe company layoffs.

E-commerce Electronic commerce. Selling goods and/or services over the Internet.

Engineering The study of putting scientific and mathematical knowledge to practical use. Typical engineering activities include planning and managing the building of bridges, dams, roads, chemical plants, machinery, and new industrial products.

Freelancer A self-employed person who handles specific jobs under contract with companies and individuals.

Fringe benefit A monetary or service bonus (such as health insurance) given to an employee in addition to regular wages or salary. Other examples of fringe benefits include performance bonuses, pension plans, paid vacations, and life insurance.

Graduate school A school that grants master's and doctorate degrees to people who have already obtained their bachelor's degrees.

Humanities The branches of learning that are concerned with language, the arts, literature, philosophy, and history. Compare **social sciences** and **natural sciences.**

Information technology (IT) Encompasses all scientific and mathematical developments that are used to create, store, and share data such as words, photographic images, motion pictures, music, and other forms of information.

Intern An advanced student (usually with at least some college training) who is employed in a job that is intended to provide supervised practical experience.

Internship 1. The position or job of an intern (see intern). 2. The period of time that a person is working as an intern.

Journeyman (or **journeyworker**) A person who has completed an apprenticeship or other training period and is qualified to work in a skilled trade.

Junior college A two-year college that offers courses similar to those in the first half of a four-year college program. Graduates usually receive an associate degree and may transfer to a four-year college or university to complete a bachelor's degree. Compare **community college.**

Liberal arts Subjects that develop broad general knowledge rather than specific occupational skills. Includes philosophy, literature, the arts, history, language, social sciences, and natural sciences.

Licensed Formal permission from the proper authority to carry out an activity that would be otherwise illegal. For example, a person must be licensed to practice medicine or to drive a car. Compare **certified.**

Life sciences The natural sciences that are concerned with living organisms and the processes that take place within them (see **natural sciences**).

Major The academic field in which a student specializes and receives a college degree.

Master's degree An academic rank or title given to a person who has completed a one- or two-year program of study beyond the bachelor's level.

Natural sciences All the sciences that are concerned with objects and processes in nature. Includes biology, chemistry, physics, astronomy, and geology. Compare **humanities** and **social sciences.**

Pension An amount of money paid regularly by an employer to a former employee after he or she retires.

Physical sciences The natural sciences that are concerned with nonliving matter. Includes physics, chemistry, and astronomy.

Private 1. Not owned or controlled by the government, such as a privately held company. 2. Intended only for a particular person or group, such as a private road or a private club.

Public 1. Provided or operated by the government, such as a public library. 2. Open and available to everyone, such as a public meeting.

Regulatory Establishing rules and laws for carrying out an activity. For example, a federal regulatory agency is a government organization that sets up required procedures for how certain things should be done.

Scholarship A gift of money to a student to help offset the cost of education.

Social sciences The branches of learning that are concerned with the behavior of groups of human beings. Includes economics and political science. Compare **humanities** and **natural sciences.**

Social studies Courses of study that deal with how human societies work. Includes civics, geography, and history.

Starting salary Salary paid to a newly hired employee, generally less than the amount paid to a more experienced worker.

Technical college Offers courses in both general and technical subjects and awards both associate degrees and bachelor's degrees. Compare **technical community college.**

Technical community college Offers courses in both general and technical subjects, but only awards associate degrees. Compare **technical college.**

Technical institute Typically offers general technical courses but does not award degrees. Technical schools that offer a broader range of subjects and award degrees are usually called technical colleges or technical community colleges.

Technical school A general term used to describe technical colleges, technical community colleges, and technical institutes. Compare **trade school** and **vocational school.**

Technician A worker with mechanical or scientific training who works under the supervision of scientists, engineers, or other profes-

sionals. Typically has two years of college-level education after high school.

Technologist A worker with specialized mechanical or scientific training who works under the supervision of scientists, engineers, or other professionals. Typically has three to four years of college-level education after high school.

Trade An occupation that involves working with one's hands. Requires specialized training and skills.

Trade school A public or private school that offers training in one or more of the skilled trades (see trade). Compare **technical school** and **vocational school.**

Undergraduate A student at a college or university who has not yet received a degree.

Undergraduate degree See **bachelor's degree.**

Union An organization of workers in a particular industry or company that works to gain better wages, benefits, and working conditions for its members. Also called a labor union or trade union.

Vocational school A public or private school that offers training in one or more skills or trades. Compare **technical school** and **trade school.**

Wage Money that is paid in return for work completed. Generally based on the number of hours or days worked.

Job Title Index

Index